TALES OF A BLACK SOJOURNER

To Sam,
Travel buddy and new
friend.

Gene Mills
Guatemala City Guatemala
July 2014

Gene Mills

TABLE OF CONTENTS

DEDICATION

This volume of stories is dedicated to the memory of my mother, Isabel Mills, whose near-silent ways of concern, care, and love I did not understand until it was much too late.

ACKNOWLDEGEMENTS

A number of years ago, I began to organize maternal family gatherings using a rental house in Hilton Head Island, South Carolina as our "headquarters". An integral part of my effort were newsletters written and distributed to family members about things, Mitchell, the surname of our grandmother, whose farm had been situated in the Armoak community less than an hour drive away. Distribution of the newsletter always brought with it several compliments, with my younger sister, Mildred Bradley, among the most frequently vocal. Coupled with newsletter compliments were also positive opinions about my vocal storytelling regarding my global travels and other past experiences. Older sister, Margaret Sessoms, joined the chorus of those making compliments. Other family members and friends later became a part of this "nudging cabal".

By and large, I felt that my friends and relatives were simply being kind to an old man. Besides which, I had never thought too much of my writing skills anyway. Then, one day, while traveling across country by train (Amtrak), a single woman was ushered to the table that I was sharing with a gentleman from West Virginia. After she was seated, I asked her the usual, where are you from and what do you do, opening gambit. When she replied that she was a free-lance travel writer my heart skipped a beat. I was enthralled to be sitting next to a REAL WRITER. With my enthusiasm at a fevered pitch, I asked my breakfast companion the really big question. How do you start writing? Her answer was stunningly simple. "Just begin writing.", she said. This conversation took place between Williams, Arizona and Los Angeles.

While I can't remember the writer's name, I took her at her word. After settling into my Los Angeles hotel room, I began to make an outline of the 20 plus stories that I wanted to tell in writing.

So, if Mildred and the other members of the "nudging cabal" had not exerted their influence, I may not have been open to the simple wisdom of the travel writer.

Too, I owe a HUGE chunk of gratitude to fellow-alumnus (Xavier University, New Orleans), Marva A. Pattillo, whose review and editing of texts both tightened up narratives and corrected glaring errors of style and grammar. The introduction she wrote for this volume nearly brought me to tears.

To each and all of you, a really big, THANK YOU! THANK YOU!

INTRODUCTION

"Life is not what one lived,

but what one remembers and

how one remembers it in order to recount it."

--Gabriel Garcia Marquez

A good story can make you think. It can stir your emotions. It can inspire hope. Some stories can do all of these as Gene Mills has demonstrated in "Tales of A Black Sojourner".

As hinted at in the title, travel is a recurring theme in the stories and black identity another. Mills has earned or been endowed with the credentials to write about both.

His passport has the stamp of dozens of foreign destinations in countries on almost every continent. Many of the trips were return visits for the second and, sometimes, the third time. Exploring the United States was not neglected. From his home base in Gainesville, Florida, and from every other location where he has lived, Mills has traveled by plane and train to find new places for learning and adventure.

It should not be surprising that black identity also has a place in the stories. In a life that unfolded during some of the most significant events in the history of African-Americans in this country, Mills understands how his racial identity affected other aspects of his 79-year journey.

"Tales of A Black Sojourner" is not an autobiography or a memoir although some of its stories have much in common with representatives of those two genres. Memoirists often focus on their authors" early years and the ordeals with family and other authority figures which framed their quests for separation and independence. Mills tells his version of that passage but he also has other kinds of stories to tell, often unrelated vignettes that describe an event, a discovery or a special occasion.

Gene Mills has an incredible memory for details about the people and events of his life. These details enrich the settings in which the stories unfold. The variety in subject matter ensures that each story can focus the reader's attention on either thinking or feeling or on hope, without neglecting other elements that contribute depth and color. Stories like "Chicago – Saudi Arabia make the reader think about what it took for Gene to find a way to keep the ever present barriers and obstructions from completely defeating him. In "Beginnings" Gene lets us join him on the emotional roller-coaster ride of his years as a small child, then as a teenager and on into his college years as he struggled, triumphed and struggled again, a pattern that continued well into adulthood.

In "Friends" you will wonder, at first, how he would find a way to survive in the face of neglect, disparagement and indifference from his parents compounded by his feelings of failure and aloneness. But he did more than survive. He thrived. And the power of friends was part of what made that possible.

"Tales of a Sojourner" includes some other great stories that will make you smile (Poor Sam! Poor Stella/J! Poor us!), sigh (Red – Green – and Black) or pray a little (The Verdict). Others will make you want to get out the atlas and start planning your visit to one – or more – of the destinations to which this book has taken you.

Marva A. Pattillo
Milwaukee Wisconsin

BEGINNINGS

The family's first house was purchased by my parents, Eugene and Isabel Mills, in the early forties after having rented the house from my mother's aunt, Nancy, for a couple of years. The house was located at 704 West Mill Street in the Porters Subdivision of Southwest Gainesville. It was within walking distance of the downtown area. Except for some edges along the perimeter, it was an all-black neighborhood. The house, like nearly all of the other houses in Porters, had wood siding and it is unclear as to the number of years that had gone by since the house had been painted. The Mills' house differed from some of the others in that brick pillars about 3 feet high formed the support for large joists beneath the wooden floors. About 7 or 8 wooden steps led from the front and back porches to the ground. This allowed breezes to circulate beneath the house bringing welcome relief from the heat and humidity of North Central Florida summers. The roof of the house was rather porous. One of my earliest memories is the ritual of placing multiple pots and pans on the floor to catch rainwater when it leaked through multiple holes in the roof during rainstorms.

There was at least one window in each room and each window was about 5 feet high. In order to keep the windows open, sticks of various kinds were needed. Windows had no screens so our bodies provided many a meal for mosquitoes that freely entered the house especially during the summer. Oddly, the house had a third porch which, unlike the others, was screened in. Besides the porous roof and unscreened windows, chinches (bedbugs) created their own set of problems. The remedy for chinches was that mattresses were sprayed occasionally with Flit or other brands of anti-critter potions.

The kitchen and dining room were situated at a 90 degree angle to the rest of the house. Access to these two rooms was accomplished through the open-sided back porch. Baths were accomplished with water heated in pots on the wood-burning kitchen stove. Sponge-offs in between full baths took place using porcelain basins and the aforementioned heated water from the same wood-burning stove. The kitchen would have more accurately been called the cooking/bathing room. Besides the wood-burning stove in the kitchen, the only other heat for colder winter months was provided by a wood-burning heater in the living room. A couple of rocking chairs and a ceiling-attached swing decorated the front porch. A huge pecan tree near the front porch steps provided shade during spring and summer. Common to the Mills' house and nearly all of the others in the neighborhood during the late 30's were outdoor toilets, kerosene lamps, and hand-operated water pumps.

This house was the place of my birth. I joined my father, mother, and a three-year old sister, Margaret, in the house at 704 West Mill Street. To call these beginnings humble would be a gross overstatement.

When I was growing up, our neighborhood was a very lively place on Friday and Saturday nights. There were two jook joints within about 20 yards of our house. Two more were located about 3 blocks away. By way of contrast, the Shady Grove Primitive Baptist Church sat next to our house. It was impossible not to hear sermons, prayers, jook music, and church music seven days per week. Added to the cacophony were sounds from The Church of

God by Faith located one block to the east of our house. Theirs was a Pentecostal congregation with many of the sounds being carried through the neighborhood well beyond the confines of the building especially since there was no air conditioning during those days and windows were open while business (church or jook) was being conducted. We could often tell when some congregant was caught up in the throes of ecstasy while testifying or speaking in tongues. Usually, the folks whom we would see entering and leaving the jook joints on weekends were not the same people whom we would see attending the two churches on Sunday mornings. Although Gainesville and Alachua County were officially dry, illegal whiskey and moonshine flowed quite freely especially in our neighborhood. As a result, and all too frequently, men and women who knew each other would get into alcohol-fueled arguments that would escalate into physical violence. Guns, knives, and fists would be used to settle differences. For instance, the step-father of a childhood friend was slain a few blocks away from our house when an argument broke out during a dice game. On another night, a guy called Tenderfoot appeared on our front porch yelling the names of my father and mother. He pleaded for my parents' help because he said that a man had shot him. Dad responded by getting up and taking Tenderfoot to Alachua General Hospital located about 10 short blocks away. Like nearly everywhere else in Gainesville and the South, facilities were separated for blacks and whites. Whether quality of services followed this division I have no direct knowledge. I do know that the "colored ward" was staffed by "colored nurses". As to Tenderfoot, we awoke the next morning to find blood all over the front porch, steps, front yard and inside my father's car. On another occasion, we were awakened by shots in the night. The next day, we found a rifle in our yard next to the forsythia hedges. One of the victims of the shooting that occurred the night before had apparently come through one side of the yard, dropped the rifle and left through the other. The victim's path could be determined because he had been bleeding and ants had built little hilly nests on the ground where blood had fallen.

Beginnings

My sister, Margaret and I could watch some of the weekend action because from our house we could look directly into the entrance of the nearest of the jook joints. It seemed that they had no volume control mechanism. The result was REALLY LOUD MUSIC until the wee hours of the morning. Besides watching the people action, we were treated to words and music of songs like; I Want to Play with Your Poodle; What's The Use of Getting Sober (When You Are Only Going to Get Drunk Again); and Gonna Move to The Outskirts of Town. Added to this mix were the competing strains of tunes from the jukebox of the second joint that was about 20 yards from our house farther down Porters Street. Needless to say, my vocabulary became much richer over the years by repeating silently some of the choice words that I frequently heard. Notice the qualifier, silently. My acquisition of such choice but forbidden words has led me to coin a phrase, "going all Porters on someone". However, to use one of the choice words in the presence of others, child or adult, and especially my mother, meant near instant death. Other neighborhood children could not be relied upon to keep such information to themselves. Disrespect of grown folks not only was forbidden but all neighbors were rewarded on the spot, practically, when reporting misbehavior to my mother.

As the saying goes, "My Mama didn't play." She pretty much ruled our home with a drill sergeant's mentality and behavior. Cleanliness and neatness of home, grounds, and person were at the top of Mama's list. Wooden porch floors and steps had to be scrubbed by hand with a scrub brush. No residue was permitted on washed dishes. Our freshly-raked dirt yard had to be free of any leaves or other debris before the job was judged to be complete. Our school clothes were always clean, smartly starched, and ironed. Indeed, clothes were washed every Monday, a practice that required three tin tubs and a boil pot. All of the water had to be pumped by hand because of the absence of city water until I was about 7 or 8 years old. The boil pot was used for heavily soiled clothes like my father's work clothes. Each piece of clothing or bedding was treated using a scrub board and either homemade lye soap or Octagon soap which was a particularly harsh commercial product. No variations of these and other standards were tolerated. During the same time period, my mother ironed on other days of the week.

Mama's fussing was usually enough to keep me in line. All too often, the fussing amounted to what is now called verbal abuse. In general, serious house rule infractions brought about instant corporal responses from Mama. Forsythia shrubs in our yard provided some of the switches used in doling out this type of punishment. Various belts rounded out the weaponry. Bared legs and arms were frequent targets. When Mama thought that my behavior was really beyond the pale, she would sic Dad on me when he came home and he would do the deed.

Because of health problems, Ma was a stay-at-home Mom. Dad worked as an automobile mechanic for Brasington Motors, the local Cadillac-Oldsmobile dealership through the late 1940's. As far as I know, no one had ever complained about either Dad's knowledge, skills, or performance in repairing either automobile motor malfunctions or body and fender damage. Based upon all available feedback, Dad was highly competent, a hard worker, and very dependable. Even though he was of draft age during World War II, his employer managed to get deferments due to his having been declared essential to the war support effort in keeping automobiles functioning during that conflict.

Despite working six days a week, Dad spent most of his evening hours away from the family home. Even decades later, I cannot speculate as to whether Dad liked his choir participation more than he did church politics or vice-versa. He sang bass/baritone well enough to perform solos during church services. He moved up in the Mount Carmel Baptist Church's governing hierarchy from board of trustees to deacon. An appropriate designation of my father's role in the politics of the Mount Carmel Baptist Church was that of gadfly. As best as I have been able to determine, my Dad was the leader of the opposition, no matter who the pastor happened to be at the time. It was not uncommon for Dad to arrive home any time between midnight and the early morning hours. To all of my mother's objections, his excuse (or lie) was always based upon church-related activities no matter whether he arrived at home near 2a.m., 3a.m., or 4a.m. Two other salient factors about Dad - he did not drink and he did not argue with my mother. Essentially, after a few words, he simply ignored her.

Dad seemed to switch mental gears once Sunday afternoon dinner was over. With little or no discussion, he would load us into the car and either visit Grampa or Aunt Eunie, or others of his relatives scattered around the same area of southeastern Alachua County. Grampa, paternal great grandfather, lived far back into the woods between Windsor and Grove Park, both near Gainesville. Visits to Grampa would result in gifts of oranges from his 20 or so trees; or collard greens from his garden; or sugar cane which we would cut from his fields depending upon the season; or eggs from his chicken coop despite the presence of an attack rooster which jealously guarded his territory. Grampa used most of his sugar cane to make syrup in the fall. Syrup-making occurred after the cane was harvested. Stalks of cane were passed through the mill, juice collected, then placed into a huge evaporation pan heated by a wood fire beneath. Margaret remembers that Grampa made homebrew from the skimmings of the evaporation pan. Homebrew was a kind of homemade firewater.

Aunt Eunie, one of Grampa's daughters, lived in Grove Park where her front porch was just a few yards away from the Gainesville-Hawthorne highway (SR 20). During some of these Sunday afternoon outings, Dad, Aunt Eunie, and one or both of her daughters, Annie Rose and Bennye Floyd, would argue with such force and volume that they could be heard far down the highway even while successfully competing with the highway traffic noise. During these gatherings, each family member thought that he or she was always right and smarter than the other. At other times, we would visit my father's Uncle Mark, Aunt Mazie , and their sons in Santos, a rural community between Ocala and Belleview in adjacent Marion County. These junkets were the most enjoyable times of the week for me outside of school hours. Those Sundays were times of discovery. It seems that I was always curious as to what was observable and unusual not only around me but just a little bit farther down the road. Also, it was a great relief to get out of the house with all of its rigid rules, tensions, fussings, and anger, as well as getting away from church with its emotionally-charged long, drawn-out services.

After Sunday evening church services ended, my Dad would occasionally stop by Dairy Queen for treats. Soft-squeeze ice cream topped with strawberries was my favorite. During such Sunday breaks, I can't recall any arguments or disagreements between my parents. It was almost as if a truce would prevail. Occasionally (probably fifth Sundays), we would be taken to American Beach, a blacks-only beach near Jacksonville. Or to St. Augustine to visit the old fort (Castillo San Marcos) or the alligator farm nearby. For some reason, the State of Florida did not view access and entry to these venues by black folks as a threat to the prevailing social order. Until this day, I still don't know what forces were at work to cause Dad to be absent from home until the wee hours of the morning, Monday thru Saturday, and become this quietly involved family man on Sundays. Was one façade real and the other not? Had he ascribed to himself a part in a drama of which only he knew all of the parts? Or were the two opposing sides of behavior simply parts of the whole?

From about age 5, my Dad had very little to say to me that was not related to some task that he wanted done or to my request for some small amount of money that I needed for school or a movie after I was in my teens. Up until the time of his death at age 93, neither my father nor I trusted each other enough to even broach the subject of his whereabouts over decades of weekday nights. Added to the mystery was Dad's practice of taking vacations by himself over the years. To say that we had a strained relationship was a massive understatement. After I was an adult, Dad offered a slight clue as to his perceptions of me and his acknowledgement of the distance that prevailed between us. At one point, he said that he had no idea how I turned out to be the somewhat successful professional that I had become because he knew that he had nothing to do with my success. Even before that he told me that I was my mother's son. I suppose that the statement somehow in his mind justified the distance which he maintained throughout my growing up years.

I kept up my end of the distance equation but I was usually angrier than hell while doing so. It seems that the idea that I had of how a father should relate to his son had absolutely nothing to do with reality. Dad's M.O. was to ignore me unless there was some compelling reason to do otherwise. For instance, he saw no reason to attend my 6th grade graduation; my 12th grade graduation, even though I had the highest grade average in my class, or my college graduation, even though I was senior class president and gave a short speech during one of the graduation ceremonies. While I was in a number of plays in elementary and high school he never bothered to attend any of them. The same thing was true for all of the band concerts of which I was a part. How do you define/describe indifference?

Mostly, the Mills household in Porters was a place of very little joy; no affection in words or deeds; and lots of resentment and anger from my mother. Dad's behavior, when he was around, seemed to be summed up as, "I work, provide money for the family, and that leaves me free to do whatever I want to do whenever I want to do it. For too long a time I felt truly alienated while living in the house. There was no way, I thought, that these people could possibly be my real parents. Despite those feelings of alienation, when it came down to taking sides when Ma fussed with Dad, I would always take her side. Arguments between parents were, therefore, very one-sided - Dad was his usual man-of-a few-words and Ma continued to fuss. He seemed, in retrospect, to be completely immunized against her emotions. This drama tended to be repeated over and over again and occur either as Dad was preparing to spend the evening elsewhere or upon his return home in the wee hours of the morning.

I do not recall a single instance growing up, where either parent affectionately touched the other. It's no wonder then that neither parent bothered to display any signs of affection towards us, the children. Margaret spent as little time in the house as she could get away with. Instead, she could be found hanging out with Big Mama (Estelle Broome), our next-door neighbor. Although the Broome family was not related to us, Big Mama's attitude towards us was just the opposite of Mama's. Big Mama was almost embarrassingly affectionate. She showered us with attention and was quite generous with her love. Hugs and kisses were quite frequent as was her quickness to brag about practically anything that we did. Her black-eye peas and lima beans were to die for. Margaret, the extrovert, was far more eclectic in her appreciation of some of the more exotic dishes that Big Mama made. I steered clear of her baked 'possum and sweet potatoes. Fried rabbit left me a bit underwhelmed and gopher tortoise or cooter, was at the top of my NOT-TO-DO list. Besides being a damn fine cook, Big Mama was fiercely protective when she thought anyone else around the neighborhood was misbehaving towards one of us. While my mother tended to be shy and non-confrontational outside of the house, Big Mama would get downright, in-your-face confrontational if she thought that there was any kind of a threat to us, the children. Big Mama and Pa Broome, her husband, never had any children. Margaret and I (and much later, younger sister Mildred) became the children that they never had. Na-na, Big Mama's mother could be relied upon for defensive back-up. While Na-na was not affectionate like Big Mama, we knew that we were really special to the Broome household.

Pa had a special name for me. He called me Sonny. Mr. Harmon Broome, Pa's real name, was an entrepreneur of sorts. He conducted a wood and parched (roasted) peanut business from his house with delivery service from his old model-T truck. I spent a lot of time helping Pa with his business by stoking the fire beneath the stand-mounted 55-gallon drum that he had converted into a peanut roaster or turning the hand crank of the drum in order to make the peanuts roast evenly. I also helped Pa measure and bag peanuts after roasting.

One of my mother's standing rules was that I could go to Big Mama's house without first getting her permission. I think that the underlying assumption was that Big Mama and Pa were highly trustworthy and that no harm would come to either Margaret or me as long as we were with the Broomes. If we caused any trouble, either Big Mama or Pa was completely free to correct the situation however he or she saw fit. Indeed, Big Mama was my mother's only friend. Ma rarely visited anyone in the neighborhood besides Big Mama unless they were sick. Even so, a number of working mothers from the neighborhood would entrust my mother with their weekly insurance premiums when the "insurance man" went door-to-door to collect. Life insurance, however modest, was important to black families because it insured that monies would be available for covering the costs of funerals and burials. My mother was quiet but well-respected in our neighborhood as was my father. The one major difference between the two was that other kids in the neighborhood felt free to talk to my mother. With some regularity, she shared our food with various kids in our neighborhood. On the other hand, when kids were playing in our yard and saw my father's car approach, they would leave and very quickly. My Dad did nothing to change their attitudes towards him. Maybe, his tendency towards maintaining an "un-smiley" face may have had something to do with their reactions.

The poverty markers that families in the neighborhood shared were outdoor toilets, lack of electricity, and running water. The outdoor toilets were serviced once a week by Mr. Stonewall who operated a tanker truck provided by the City of Gainesville. He visited each toilet, removed the waste buckets, and transferred contents to the tanker truck. None of the streets in Porters was paved during this time. Instead, there was this thick grayish sand that could wreak havoc with vehicles trying to negotiate passage through any of the streets during or immediately after a hard rain. Of course, storm drains were out of the question. The nearby ice plant sold ice in increments of 25 pounds. Until electricity was made more widely available to the neighborhood, most families would have to designate someone to make the trip to buy and transport ice so that food in ice boxes would be kept cool. From the age of 7 or 8, I was our family's designated person. It is clear, now, that there was a very practical reason for my parents to have given me a red wagon for a Christmas present. The wagon allowed me to play the role of family ice boy. It was very helpful that the ice plant platform was manned by Reverend James Shannon, a man who had roomed at our house during the late thirties until he married Miss Fanny Ballard.

Despite the level of poverty in Porters during my early years, about half of the houses nearest ours were owned by the families living in them. Most of the others were owned by white landlords. Even so, yards were frequently raked and kept pretty neat as I remember. The occasional neighborhood empty lot was not a place where people discarded trash. On the contrary, there was one empty lot in particular that was practically covered in wild flowers during the spring - phlox of various colors, black-eyed susans, and a kind of small pink lily. Remnants of an old house on the lot were covered in blue wisteria for a short period during the spring. Automobile ownership, including trucks, was less common. Of the 30 or so homes in Porters, maybe a third of the families owned vehicles. Families who did not own vehicles either walked to work, or church, or the grocery store unless they caught a ride with someone else. It was not uncommon, for instance, for whites to visit the neighborhood in order to pick up and drop off women who worked in their homes as domestics. Similarly, farm owners would drive or send trucks into Porters in order to pick up and drop off folks who worked in the fields around Gainesville and other parts of Alachua County. For a while, telephone ownership was very rare. I believe that Miz Stella Knowles was the only neighbor who had a telephone.

Miz Stella was considered to be the most well-off person around. She was a black business lady who owned a rental house and the jook joint next to her house. Not only did she own her home and car, she had a chauffeur to drive her around. Rumor had it that she conducted still another business from her home that may have caused a problem or two with legal authorities. After all, Gainesville and all of Alachua County were "dry".

Web-based Rand McNally's distance calculator measures the distance between our house and Williams Elementary School as being 1.2 miles. I was really surprised at that figure because it always felt much farther than that. Joseph Williams Elementary School was my second school at age 6 after having spent a year of kindergarten at St. Augustine (Episcopal) School located in what is now The Fifth Avenue-Mt. Pleasant District. Like everything else in Gainesville and throughout the South during that time, racial segregation was the law. Not only did whites consider blacks to be inferior, there were reminders all over the place. Bathrooms in public spaces were always segregated with signs that clearly designated the race that was permitted within. "White Only". "Colored". These were examples of reminders to blacks of our perceived inferior status. Some restaurants permitted blacks to purchase food provided that they conducted business through an exterior window usually found in the rear of the establishment. Quite common if not universal was the practice that forced blacks to use the back door of any white person's home while either entering or leaving as a domestic or making a delivery. Water fountains in stores and government buildings were always labeled and separate. White students on Alachua County school busses would pass us as we trudged to Williams. Common were shouts of "Nigger! Nigger! Nigger!" by those being bussed. Not exactly a great way to start a school day. Then there was a white man named D.A. Smith who lived on Depot Street about 3 blocks from our house. He would occasionally order his dogs to chase us as we passed his house on the way to or from Williams. It seems that he thought that it was great sport to have his dogs harass us despite the fact that we were all of elementary school age. I can't remember if any black kids were actually bitten during those times. A far more personal incident happened to me one day when I was about 4 or 5. My mother had given me money to go and buy a loaf of bread from a small grocery store a block away. The store was owned by a white man whom we called Mr. Pinky. My mother had always taught us to be polite, especially to grown (adult) people. On entering the store, I saw a second white man standing in front of the counter. I waited patiently to give Mr. Pinky my request but before I did, the second white man looked down at me and said, "Pinky, why don't we cut this little nigger's nuts off?" Since I was all of 4 or 5 years old at the time, I wasn't quite sure what or where my nuts were but I was smart enough to know that I had them and that here was a threat that I was going to lose them at the hands of this white man's knife. I left that store in a flash and ran all the way back home without the loaf of bread. I remember breathlessly telling my mother what happened but I don't remember her reaction. What is certain is that she neither said nor did anything of a confrontational nature. Neighborhood conventional wisdom declared that under such circumstances, you sucked up such threats and abuse and moved on as best as you could given the circumstances. Talking back or speaking up to a white person could lead to really serious trouble if you were black. Such behavior was considered uppity, disrespectful, and totally unacceptable. Oddly, I have no memory of any discussions that were ever held in any of my classes in elementary or high school that addressed this vast Southern system of social apartheid, inequality, and abuse. When whites would refer to elderly blacks as "auntie" or "uncle" or "preacher" or "deacon" as they frequently did, the underlying assumptions were that such elderly black folks were non-threatening, inferior, respectful of white superiority and clearly knew their place in the larger social order of the times.

Another incident occurred when I was about 9 years old. My Dad had driven to my grandmother's farm in South Carolina in order to bring Margaret and me back to Gainesville after my mother had given birth to my younger sister, Mildred. It had been a difficult birth that lasted many hours. Ma was in South Carolina because she was not sure that she would survive childbirth after having had a kidney removed the year before. I was in bed in an adjacent room while the whole birthing thing was going on. The noises scared hell out of me. Like many others during those times, it was a home birth attended to by Miz Ada, a local black midwife. At any rate, my parents had decided that Ma needed more time in South Carolina in order to recover. So, on the day of our departure from Armoak, my Dad drove with Margaret and me all the way south to Jessup Georgia and decided that he needed to stop for gas. While the white gas station attendant was filling up, I asked Dad if I could get a soda from the restaurant inside. Dad, in turn, asked the attendant if that would be o.k. and he said yes. With Dad's ok, I went inside and stood respectfully and silently at the end of the counter (I already knew that I could not sit.). When asked by the counter man what I wanted, and I replied that I wanted an orange soda, he said, "We don't serve niggers in here." I was 10 years old at the time. Needless to say, I went back to the car embarrassed and told my Dad what happened. I waited until we got back to Gainesville in order to have that orange soda. As with the incident with Mr. Pinky, it was clear that neither parent could protect me from the prevailing hatred, disdain, and overall consequences of government-mandated racial segregation nor racist attitudes and abusive behaviors. Black institutions provided some temporary havens from this kind of oppression. For many of us, dealing with white people always carried with it a kind of pervasive but unspoken fear. If you were deemed to not know your place as a black person, or otherwise seemed to be insufficiently subservient, the white could simply make up a story and either the formal or informal justice system would deal with you and probably harshly no matter what the reality was.

Beginnings

For me, school was my haven. At age 5, Ma had the wisdom to enroll me in the St. Augustine Episcopal School for kindergarten. In addition, she made an arrangement with Mrs. Sarah Young, Chester Williams' grandmother, to have Chester escort me to school because he was a bit older and was also a student at St. Augustine. Ma would walk with me to the Williams' house about four blocks away and Chester would walk with me to and from school. It is unclear why Ma took these steps. A cynic might conclude that it was convenient to get me out of the house for a few hours. After all, I could be a pretty whiny little dude whose feelings were easily hurt. I was also quiet, shy, and developed a love for reading. (The word, nerd, would have been somewhat applicable). Besides which, Ma shared the belief that children should be seen and not heard. I do believe now, that in these actions was a tacit acknowledgement that school was very important.

While there were no overt messages to me from either parent regarding the need and value of education, I found out in first grade that being obedient and striving to excel were two keys to affection, respect and praise from my teachers and some of my classmates. From then on, I modeled my in-school behavior in a way that would keep the stream flowing. In some ways, I felt like the plant in the movie, Little Shop of Horrors. FEED ME! FEED ME! I came to idolize my teachers and even developed a crush on a few of them. If a teacher had told me that I should pick up and bring our house to school the very next day, I would have gone home and told my mother (even nag her) that I had to pick up our house and bring it to school the very next day. While I did not consider and have never felt that I was particularly bright, my first grade experiences steered me into circumstances in which I quietly screamed for more and more positively oriented attention. Fortunately for me, Ms. Lang, supervisor of "Negro Education" for Alachua County, started a practice that was right down my alley. With permission from my mother and the cooperation of our first grade teacher, Ms. Thelma Jordan, Ms. Lang would come to Williams Elementary, pick 3 or 4 of us who were deemed to be top performers in our classroom and take us to faculty meetings in outlying black elementary schools around the county. She would have us do a kind of dog and pony show, demonstrating our newly acquired knowledge and skills. After our demonstrations were concluded and the faculty meetings were over, my fellow students and I would be treated to all kinds of goodies like hot cocoa, delicious baked beans, and exotic (for us) hot dogs. Oh man! It couldn't get any better than that. I can't remember whether Ms. Lang or any of those faculty members ever asked us any questions during our dog and pony shows. I do remember, however, the joy of being singled out as one of the better students in my class. From those experiences in first grade through the rest of my 21 or so years pursuing a diploma and academic degrees, getting good grades was always paramount. Full disclosure: I flunked out of my first attempt at graduate school (St. John's University College of Pharmacy, New York City) because I had conflicts in setting priorities. I didn't see why I had to choose between partying on weekends, studying, and working full-time across a six-day week while spending about three hours a day commuting. Partying won that round. Unhelpful was the reality of my coursework - calculus, graduate biochemistry, reading French, and a seminar in which each student was required to prepare and present a research paper during the term. Because of my lack of priorities, I was instructed to never darken the doors of St. John's University ever again.

From first grade on, I would do whatever I could to get to school and on time. On one occasion when I was 6 or 7, rain was coming down pretty heavily when it was time for me to leave for school. Because I had neither raincoat nor umbrella, my mother insisted that I wait until the rain stopped. Oh boy! My tears started flowing. I tried to impress upon my mother why it was so important that I get to school and on time. As always, Ma won that argument too.

You see, there was a kind of contradiction going on. Among my mother's many traits, she had great disdain for what she called mannish or womanish kids. "Back talk" was not permitted. Any sentence that started with the words, "Well, Mama" always brought an immediate and angry response, "Don't well me!" Sometimes, "Well, Mama" got your face slapped. One of her other immediately silencing expressions when things got dicey between us was the question, "You think you're grown, huh?" Of course, the only acceptable answer to such a rhetorical question was, "No ma'am."

I am grateful to my aunt Nellie, my father's older sister, for having given me my first taste of semi-independence and adventure at age five. She took me to spend a couple of weeks with her and Uncle Henry, her husband. They lived in a small house on Cow Pen Lake in Putnam County Florida, about twenty or so miles away from Gainesville. I think that their house and property were owned by Kaola Clay Mine, Uncle Henry's employer. In order to get to the house, you had to travel along a very sandy dirt road through piney woods about a mile or so distant from the Gainesville-Palatka highway, State Road 20 again. Both aunt and uncle worked full-time away from the house so I was left to fend for and entertain myself while they worked. Fortunately, I was allowed to bring my dog, Spot, with me. (OK. Naming my dog Spot didn't say much about my level of imagination or creativity. The dog was white with black spots.) My dog and I spent nearly all of my unsupervised time exploring the woods and lakeside near the house. I found and picked wild huckleberries whenever I could find them. Wild blackberries were also among my favorites.

Unfortunately, I also discovered red bugs, also known as chiggers. On one of the days of my many discovery missions on Cow Pen Lake, I wound up with an infestation of red bug bites mainly on my chest. My chest was particularly vulnerable because my mother and my aunt forgot to send/bring extra clothes for me to wear while I was visiting. Aunt Nellie decided that it was not necessary to go back to Gainesville for my clothes because she could make a pair of pants for me. After one or two nights, I was the proud owner of a pair of bibbed-overalls made from old flour sacks which Aunt Nellie had been saving. So, for two weeks or so, I roamed around the woods near Cow Pen Lake in my off-white homemade flour sack bibbed-overalls without a shirt. Spot didn't mind and I didn't either. The red bugs appreciated the exposure. Conditions were ideal for them. Not ideal, however, were the redness and itching on my chest of such intensity that I probably created a new dance that probably could not be choreographed by anyone else. The night of my exposure brought about a treatment from Aunt Nellie - a bath in kerosene. It worked. For some reason, Spot was spared and did not share in my exposure and infestation. Maybe he knew something that I didn't know. After all, he did not eat huckleberries. I also discovered something else that Spot knew instinctively that I did not know. He knew that he could swim. So, while Uncle Henry and I were fishing in the lake, Spot jumped from the boat. I was so upset that I was going to jump into the lake to save him without knowing how to swim. Uncle Henry said something profound like, "Sit down, you damn fool! The dog knows how to swim!" That order brought a quick end to my hysteria. Spot very quietly swam back to the boat.

When I was around 9 years old, my mother became very ill and had to be hospitalized. It was decided that I would spend the remainder of the summer of that year with Aunt Nellie and Uncle Henry. They never had kids of their own. At that time they had relocated to and both worked for Harry P. Leu, a very well-to-do businessman, and his wife who lived on a 50-acre estate on the northern end of Orlando Florida (before Disney). My aunt was the cook and my uncle was one of three groundskeepers. During my Orlando stay of several weeks, I was left alone from early morning to late afternoon while my aunt and uncle worked. They lived on the estate grounds in one of three houses made available to the help. The estate grounds were like this wonderful new world of discovery for me. I entertained myself by endlessly wandering around while examining the plant and animal life within the estate grounds. Occasionally, I would pretend that I was Tarzan or some other fictional super-hero. Instead of a jungle, the Leu citrus groves provided my imaginary action background. Besides oranges, grapefruit, kumquats, and tangelos, there were also camellias, azaleas, hibiscus, and roses mixed in among the citrus trees. Peacocks wandered the property freely. There was a hot-house in which were pineapples, papayas, coffee plants, and other non-native fruits. At the eastern edge of the property was a very long cage sub-divided into smaller sections. The cages held many kinds of exotic birds from different sections of the world. I never seemed to tire of this magnificent sight. The variety of colors, sizes, and other characteristics were truly amazing. The profound ways in which those weeks in Orlando affected me still bring a smile to my face. Indeed, I caught my first fish, unsupervised, while fishing from the Leu's dock.

While growing up in our household, I cannot remember a single instance in which either parent complimented me on doing a good job in school even though I was either the best student in my class or one of the best. The lone exception to my successes was high school physical education which I hated and performed accordingly. To me, it was a subject devoid of learning opportunities. Worse yet, this playtime hour consisted of unsupervised games of softball or touch football in which I had zero interest. In eighth grade, I found my new love, music. I got my parent's permission to join the high school band. School administration decided that band could be an acceptable alternative to those boring hours of unsupervised game playing. YAAY! While I was lousy as a student of music theory and instrumental proficiency I became good enough at playing the mellophone or E flat horn that I avoided the terrible wrath, rages, and tantrums of our band director, Jerry Miller. At times, Mr. Miller's displeasures and tantrums would lead to violently snapped batons, upended music stands, screaming, and sheets of music torn to shreds. Those outbursts were a sight to behold! Oh, but the sheer joy of making music together far outweighed moments of Jerry Miller's temporary insanity. Jerry worked our asses off both in marching season (read football game performances) and concert season. Of the two, I liked concert season best. We got to perform music of really serious composers of the likes of J.S. Bach, Brahms, von Suppe, and Wagner. Fortunately, we had a few really great musicians in our midst during those years. A number of names come to mind: my classmate Lawrence Rizor, Wilton and Bill Hendrix, brothers Henry and Mervin Jones, Carlton Lattimore, and Yvonne Henry. In a sense, instead of having been saved by the bell, I was saved (from phys. Ed.) by the baton.

As previously mentioned, I sought out the approval of my teachers and liked (craved?) the positive attention of my teachers and classmates. In this regard, I tried very hard to be a kind of model student in my grades, classroom participation, and deportment. The unenlightened may have viewed my behavior as that of sucking up to my teachers. I , on the other hand, was on a mission in which the payoff was affection and approval. By contrast, despite bringing home report cards filled with lots of A's and B's, I cannot recall an instance in which either parent ever made a single comment to me, not even a negative one that had to do with my report cards. This silence seemed to say to me that I was no one special and at best, my presence in the family was only tolerated and had no other significance. There was only one instance in which I recall that my father expressed any interest in my academic status. That occurred in my senior year at Xavier University while enrolled in the College of Pharmacy. It was the week before first semester finals and I became fearful that I was not going to make it. Exhaustion and feelings of being overwhelmed characterized my emotional state. Besides cleaning floors in the University's cafeteria every night, Monday thru Friday, I also acted as a kind of assistant editor of our class yearbook, actively participated in student government, and was also senior class president. Twenty-two semester hours of academic course work were also a part of the mix. On Sundays, I spent the day working in Boutte's Pharmacy on S. Galvez St. in New Orleans. I assisted the pharmacist brothers in compounding prescriptions; I cleaned floors; manned the soda fountain (was a part-time soda-jerk); and did anything else that the owners demanded of me. For all of this varied pharmacy activity, I received the ripe sum of $5.00 per Sunday. Of course, I was responsible for covering the costs of bus fare from Xavier's campus to Boutte's Pharmacy.

Until this day, even at age 78, it still smarts that neither of my parents were encouraging in my scholastic pursuits. While I don't BLAME them that I was not even more successful academically, I have often wondered what I might have become if I had had some emotional support during my formative years. Alas, the mystery will forever remain so.

Unfortunately, I incorporated my mother's frequent message to me in some part of my brain that I was lazy and would never amount to anything. By contrast, I started working for pay when I was about 6 years old and Henry Grant, barber and cousin-in-law, hired me to sweep his barbershop floor for about 25 cents a week. It was fortunate that his barbershop was just across Porters Street from our house. My next paid gig was cleaning the house of the Calhoun family during the summer around age 7. My next paid job the following summer was cleaning the home of the Sheelly (sp?) family next door to the Calhouns. A year or so later, I delivered (by bike) orders from Canova Drugstore. Employment at McCollum's Drugstore and the Gainesville Chamber of Commerce followed before I was 14. Either Florida had no child labor laws during those years or the laws were deemed to be irrelevant. I think that my disastrous experience at St. John's University was a way of fulfilling my mother's prediction about me in that I was lazy and would never amount to anything. See, Mama, I can fail as disastrously as the next person. I've become exactly what you frequently predicted. What I did not realize until many years later was that my mother worked quietly behind the scene in amassing and providing material support for my somewhat modest academic pursuits. She simply never told me what she was doing. My more silent and distant father went along with Ma's direction. After all, Dad, despite his emotional distance and self-centeredness in many ways, entrusted Ma with the family's finances. My university fees and tuition were always paid and on time. All during my 4 years at Xavier, I was always reluctant to write home and ask for anything that was not absolutely required. Telephone calls were expensive in my mind and I only recall one instance in which I actually called home. In some ways, maybe I was becoming frugal like my mother.

I think my mother's yelling at me for various perceived offenses and her predictions that I would never amount to anything had more to do with taking out her frustrations, anger, and unhappiness on me because I happened to be the most readily available target. When she was not being supercritical of me, she treated me as an ally because I took her side regarding my father's seeming indifference and stories from others as to who my father was screwing on the side. Such was the case, for instance, in which my Dad insisted that Ma cook enough to accommodate the piano player for his choir, choir number 2, for Sunday dinner. Coupled with my Dad's early morning arrivals on occasions in which he claimed that he had to take the piano player to her home in High Springs after choir rehearsal, I felt that the occasion was his most dastardly act in which he showed his disdain for Ma and the rest of us, the family. Added to the mix earlier was a rumor that the son of another pianist for choir number 2 was actually my father's child. The child was a year or so younger than my younger sister, Mildred.

Despite all of my hang ups (Does anyone else use this phrase anymore?), disappointments, failures, mental confusion, and inner chaos, the one thing that has remained fairly consistent, is the sense of curiosity that forms the basis of my many and varied travels. I attribute my early visits with Aunt Nellie and the Sunday excursions led by my Dad as two factors which helped to form and feed the travel bug. Those early experiences provided a kind of escape valve from the unhappiness surrounding our home life while I was growing up. Still needing an escape from some of the shadows, I've become a little more sophisticated. Over the past several decades I have spent a lot of time searching for and planning my next destination. Experience has taught me that I tend to really come alive and reveal more of my true self when I travel whether the travel takes place abroad or on a cross-country train trip. Of late, I have come to realize that a switch clicks on when I am traveling in a group or even on a cross-country train trip. I really enjoy talking to other people. My reception and interactions with many people tend to become self-validating experiences that I sorely missed growing up in my family's home. It has taken me a long time to realize that speaking of my past may be of interest to more than a few people, hence this and other stories in this volume.

It is now my custom to say a prayer of thanksgiving for the gifts which I have been given. My life has been greatly enriched since I have uncovered the practice of gratitude. I believe this practice has brought me to a life more rewarding than it would have been had I chosen a different path in light of the emotional baggage that I allowed myself to accumulate over the years. Thank you for these gifts, Mother-Father, God.

DOWN MEXICO WAY

My one year of high school Spanish had been a lot of fun. Part of the fun was using Spanish with other members of the class to say mysterious things in front of fellow-students who were not in The Club of Spanish Learners. Okay, it was snobbish and elitist, sort of, but oh so much fun. Unfortunately, the "geniuses" of the all-white Alachua County school board who made decisions regarding curricula, especially at "negro" or "colored" schools, decided that my high school (Lincoln High) would not offer second year Spanish because an insufficient number of students had signed up for the offering. Because the rug had been snatched from beneath my feet, I developed and retained this nagging feeling of being incomplete when it came to Spanish. It was with the desire to return to fun Spanish-learning stuff that I registered for a beginning Spanish class offered by the community education program of New York University.

At some point during the year, Mr. Wolff (I think that his first name was Gerald) circulated a brochure describing a trip to Mexico and Guatemala that he was going to lead in the summer. The possibility definitely spiked my interest. I signed up for the two-week Mexico portion of the trip because that was the maximum length of time that I could take off from work. I paid for the trip and waited impatiently for the date of departure to arrive. In the meantime, I began speaking glowingly about the trip to my ski buddy, Alan, a Ph.D. chemist from the U.K. He decided that he wanted in also and signed up.

At some point later, I received word that Gerald Wolff was cancelling his involvement. However, if I still wanted to go, arrangements would be made for a guide/driver to provide transport to all of the sites previously listed in the itinerary. That would include Mexico City, Taxco, Oaxaca, and Acapulco. I said yes.

My adventure really started at the airport on the evening of departure from New York City to Mexico City. According to the young man at the airline check-in counter, I was the last person to check in for the flight. He asked whether I wanted to travel first class. I responded negatively and added that I simply could not afford the cost. His retort went something like this. "Sir, I did not ask you whether you could afford to fly first class. I asked you whether you wanted to fly first class." Well, of course I wanted to fly first class without having to pay for the upgrade. He assigned me to a seat next to a Mexican United Nations diplomat.

The airline (I think that it was Aeronaves de Mexico) did not scrimp on either food or booze while attending to its first class passengers. I lost track of the numbers of apertifs, glasses of wine, liquers, etc. that I had and it all started while we were still on the tarmac. A sober person might have been a tad concerned, for instance, when it took nearly 20 minutes or so to get the aircraft door closed and secured. There was an awful lot of banging in attempts to secure the door. But this hero was not perturbed. They had to secure the door or the plane could not take off. Right? So no need to be alarmed.

The more I drank the greater the risk that the diplomat would be talked to death. As I recall, the core of our conversation was about Cuba and global politics. Comparable to a fine BMW, or Porsche, I went from zero to 60 in a few seconds, with zero representing shy introversion and to 60 being an over-talkative boor. Poor diplomat. Finally after dinner service was over, he said that he was tired and needed to sleep. He added that, perhaps, we could continue our discussion the next day in Mexico City, whereupon he handed me his card. Message, I am tired of your yakking. Give me a break, please! Silence prevailed over our seats for the balance of the flight. I may have been inebriated but I wasn't stupid, at least not that time. While I don't remember which individual picked me up from the airport, I did arrive safely at a small hotel near the Paseo de La Reforma.

The next morning, I left the hotel and found a restaurant where I could have breakfast. In making my selection from the Spanish-language only menu, I somehow managed to confuse huevos rancheros with huevos revueltos. What I wanted was scrambled eggs. The dish that I received had two eggs, softly fried, sunny side up with red chili sauce on top. The thought of eating what looked like two bloodied eyeballs was not at all appealing.

While eating breakfast, I noticed a balding but young man seated at the same counter a few stools away. In English, he asked me where I was from. We struck up a conversation. He said that he was Mickey Braffet, a former U.S. Marine, working then as a Revlon salesperson in San Diego California. Later, while waiting in the hotel lobby for something that I cannot remember, I noticed that there was a young man sort of hanging back a bit from a group of aging females. Somehow, we began a conversation. He said that his name was Buzz, a state legislator from Illinois, who had come down to Mexico for some kind of U.N.-related trip. He was with the group of ladies which included his aunt. I think that it was for dinner that Buzz, Mickey, and I (Los Tres Amigos) decided to walk down from the hotel towards the Zocalo, the proverbial heart of Mexico City, while looking for a place to eat.

While walking along La Reforma, we noticed a number of men standing or moving around parked cars, occasionally speaking to male pedestrians passing by. The basic question seemed to be, "Would you like to have some fun?" It became obvious that these were men who were soliciting business for various houses of ill repute. It seemed that there was a law that prevented women from soliciting business on the street. After dinner, on our return through the same location, one man became a little more aggressive than the others. We stopped after he presented his business card. Printed on the face of the card was the name Blackie Chavez, his taxi stand number, and the phrase, "One for fun, fun for all." Blackie wanted to make a deal with us (all in near perfect English). He told us that he and his driver would take us to the house which he represented. We would be under no obligation to participate in any of the activities of the house and they would bring us right back to the area of his taxi stand. Suddenly, Los Tres Amigos were in a situation in which no one wanted to chicken out. We agreed to the terms of the verbal agreement and got into the rear seat of Blackie Chavez's taxi.

As we drove farther and farther away from La Reforma, a stab of fear pierced our adventurous mindsets. Suppose we were being set up for a robbery? An image flashed in my mind of the front page of the New York Daily News. Three American Tourists Found Robbed and Murdered in Mexico City.

After winding its way through the streets of a nearly darkened neighborhood, the car came to a stop. We followed along behind Blackie as he approached a doorway. We could barely see the outline of a man sitting on the steps leading to the doorway. As we got closer, the man rose and opened the door. The entry hallway was not well-lit but we could hear strains of music coming from somewhere inside of the house. The hallway gave way to a large well-lit room in which there were a number of seats, some of which were occupied by various individuals. The seats that we chose were adjacent to the wall opposite the entryway of the big room. Nearby was a bar and a stairwell leading up to a second floor where, presumably, the real business of the house took place. Periodically, a drunken man would appear with arms draped around a young woman as they navigated the stairs. The phrase, sloppy seconds, suddenly popped into my head and the idea of screwing a woman who had been pawed over by a drunken man was nearly stomach-churning.

Shortly after being seated, Buzz, Mickey and I put our heads together and came up with a survival strategy. We would order drinks to show our good faith but we would not partake of other services. This we did. What to make of my first visit to a brothel? A whorehouse? A cathouse? Oh, if my mother could see me now.

Soon, about seven or eight young women arrived and arrayed themselves in front of us. We let them know that our interests were of the curiosity kind and perhaps, we would return at a later date. All but one of the group dispersed. While I can't remember the name that she gave us, what I do remember pretty clearly was the remaining young woman's decision to mess with Mickey. She came and sat near him and they started bantering back and forth. At one point, she asked Mickey for $10. When he said no, she responded that she would make a deal with him. If he was packing more than 10 inches in his trousers, she would pay him $10. Mickey's response was that he didn't want to take her money.

I guess that the young woman tired of the game so she rose and left our non-participating selves.

Soon, we also tired of the scene. Somehow Blackie materialized and he brought us back to the taxi stand just as he had promised. We three middle-class Americans put ourselves at great risk by getting into Blackie Chavez's car not knowing where the hell we were going nor how trustworthy Blackie and his driver were. There is that expression that the good Lord takes care of babies and fools. Neither of the three of us had been babies for a very long time.

During my stay in Mexico City, I got around to visiting quite a few of the tourist spots: The Floating Gardens of Xochimilco; Chapultepec Park; the famous murals of Rivera, Orozco, and Siquieros in the Palace of Fine Arts; and a performance of the Ballet Folklorico. I even spent a fair amount of time walking in Alameda Park or sitting while people watching. Dinner on the 37th floor of El Torre Latino Americano (the Latin American Tower) sort of rounded out the experiences. I do remember that Alan had caught up with us by then because we had dinner together there. The views from any window of the restaurant were outstanding.

Our next destination was Acapulco with a stop in Taxco, home of an old silver mine. The guide/driver's name was Perfecto, an American who had not only been living in Mexico for a couple of decades, but was also married to a Mexican lady. In response to my stated desire to learn to speak Spanish, he informed me during the drive that the best way to learn Spanish was to marry a woman who spoke the language. Seated in the front seat next to Perfecto were two young women from Chile. They both kept turning around to stare at me as I sat in the backseat. The fact that each of them smiled during such times made their stares a bit more acceptable. Finally, I asked Perfecto to ask the ladies why they kept staring. The answer was very surprising. They said that they had never seen a black man before as there was none in their home-country, Chile. (This encounter took place around 1959 or 1960.) I can't remember what my reaction was. A few years later during a trip to Chile, I found out that they were not lying.

The most exciting thing that I remember from Acapulco was La Quebrada (gulch or ravine). Divers stood on a cliff and plunged many feet below into the ocean amidst rocks and giant boulders. The timing had to be just right or we might have seen a fatal case of diver-on-the rocks. That these young men would risk their lives in such a dangerous way for the entertainment of tourists was a bit mind-blowing. The landscape as viewed from the beach was impressive especially against the mountainous terrain that formed a backdrop for all of the high rise buildings situated along the beach.

After spending a couple of days in Acapulco, we continued on to Oaxaca. I cannot remember how we traveled from Acapulco to Oaxaca. Because of a few twists Oaxaca was far more memorable than was Acapulco. First of all, there were the ruins of Mitla and Monte Alban. No details of those sites stand out in my mind decades later. On one of the tours, there were just three of us - a New Yorker named Helen Kruger, Alan, and I. The driver said that his name was Jorge or George in English. He told us that he would be our guide/driver for the remainder of our time in Oaxaca and we agreed upon a fee. Further, he added, he was pure Zapotec. The Zapotecs are an indigenous group that has been in the Oaxaca area for centuries. According to a Wikipedia entry, Zapotecs built the cities of Mitla and Monte Alban. Jorge's English was not very good so Helen and I would try to fill in when we were at a language impasse. Helen spoke some Spanish which was very helpful. I could speak a few sentences in Spanish also. Alan on the other hand spoke no Spanish at all.

Somewhere in the mix of scheduled and unscheduled trips, the notion of a nightclub visit came up. The four of us agreed that Jorge would pick us up that evening and take us to a nightclub. As we traveled away from our hotel, we began to sing songs in Spanish and crack jokes, etc., leaving Alan in the dark but a lot of fun for the others of us. We finally arrived at the end of the road and saw this closed wide wooden gate in front of us. Jorge approached the gate and someone on the other side slid back a mini-door that was about face high. A couple of words were passed and the larger door swung open to allow our entry. Did this "nightclub" operate as some kind of illegal speakeasy? Why was the secrecy necessary? As we walked further onto the property, I noticed that the single building was constructed like a U. Several doors were situated around the U and opened onto the open space between. By now, I'm getting even more suspicious. We finally walk into a brightly lit room where there were several tables and chairs and a juke box. A few young ladies sat among the tables either separately or in small groups of two or more. This scenario suggested only one possibility in my mind. I turned to Jorge and asked in Spanish, Es esta la casa de las viejas? (Is this the house of the old ladies? literally) Okay, this wasn't exactly correct Spanish, maybe) Jorge had a one-word response, "Si." I cracked up and turned to Helen and asked her if she knew the real nature of the business of this establishment? She looked around, puzzled. I let her know that she had been brought to a whorehouse by none other than our trusted driver, Jorge. What a picture! Two men and a woman brought into a cathouse by a local and apparently well-known driver.

Indeed, after we were seated for a while, a woman (attractive and smiling) came over to our table and Jorge introduced her as his "wife". The easy-going nature of the talk between them suggested that they REALLY KNEW each other. When I suggested to Helen that she would not be able to tell her New York friends about this little episode, she said, "You really don't know my friends." Apparently, her friends would probably have enjoyed the event as much she did while experiencing it. It took a few minutes for Helen to stop laughing after she found out the kind of place that we were visiting. I can't remember what Alan's response was. I guess that I was too busy laughing to notice his reaction.

Another people issue arose in Oaxaca. Buzz, his aunt and her group arrived in Oaxaca and at the same hotel where we were staying. While the combined group was standing in front of a statue of Benito Juarez, a national Mexican hero, and the guide was giving a spiel on Juarez's contribution, one of the ladies in Buzz's group raised her hand. After being recognized by the local guide whose spiel she had interrupted, she said, "We can read about this in our guidebooks. We want to go shopping." I was embarrassed and turned to Buzz and quietly expressed my amazement at the rudeness of the interruption. He told me that the interrupting lady was his aunt. OOPS! Pardon me while I extract foot from mouth, please!

Later on during the day, Alan, Buzz, and I were in the bar and we began to talk about booze and our respective capacities. I had picked up an 8oz. bottle of mescal from somewhere. Surely, I must have already been inebriated because I bet $10, I think it was, that I could chug-a-lug all 8oz without stopping. I don't think that there was a worm in my bottle as was often the custom with mescal. For those not familiar with mescal, it is distilled from the maguey plant just as tequila is distilled from the blue agave plant (per

Wikipedia). Unfortunately, the taste reminded me of trying to drink a half-pint of smoky castor oil laced with alcohol. Despite such impediments, I won the $10 bet. Unfortunately, I paid a much higher price for my indulgence. I was sick with gastrointestinal problems for two days after my victory. Never tried that stunt again.

The bottom line is that I thoroughly enjoyed my first trip to Mexico. While I found the post-colonial history of the country to be confusing and difficult for me to digest and remember (I have the same problem even with U.S. history.) I thoroughly enjoyed the people whom I met. There was something pleasantly challenging in trying to dig around in my memory bank for a Spanish word or phrase that would be apt for the moment. My sense of humor even back then tended to bounce between the impish to slightly cynical and droll. (Had to look that word up.) I was all too eager to participate in any discussion going on around me that would allow me to assume the role of smartass. Ah, but the power of the murals of The Big Three - Rivera, Orozco, and Siquieros. I don't remember how much time that I spent standing before each muralist's work trying to absorb the intended message. This was a pleasure that I thoroughly enjoyed all by myself. If the truth were known, the quality of this experience in the presence of others would have been lessened for sure. Here are some other lessons learned from my first trip. STAY THE HELL AWAY FROM MESCAL! Even without the worm, it can do great bodily harm. Mexican rose wines were fruity and delicious. Mexican food and I had not yet become best buds. That would come about a couple of decades later. I failed to heed Perfecto's advice because neither of my marriages was to a Spanish-speaking woman which probably explains why I continue to retake beginning Spanish classes over and over and over again. Pillow-talk in Spanish would have taken care of this problem and kept me out of divorce court, maybe.

CARIBBEAN CAPERS

Okay. I'll admit it. The title is meant to deceive. It was chosen to convey naughtiness and skinny-dipping in the moonlight and rum-soaked nights chasing nubile maidens across brilliant white sandy beaches (Yeah, you can too really see white sands in the moonlight). Alas! I have no such ribald Caribbean stories to tell. Well, almost none.

My first trip to the Caribbean coincided with my first trip outside of the continental United States. While I cannot accurately recall what motivated me to choose Puerto Rico and St. Thomas as my first trips abroad, the decision may have depended primarily upon my meager financial assets at the time. I was a somewhat newly licensed pharmacist employed at Lenox Hill Hospital in Manhattan. In either 1959 or 1960, I decided that my salary of $90 per week was sufficient to cover essential living expenses and about 10 days split between the two islands. Besides, the affordability issue, there had to have been some local chatter about the attractive nature of the beaches, the enjoyment of which could be enhanced through the liberal intake of cheap island-made rum. Here was my first golden opportunity to live the high life even if only for a few days. Thus, on the evening of my departure, I took a San Juan-bound American Airlines flight out of New York's JFK Airport (once Idlewild). It was an evening flight characterized by a darkened cabin and lots of screaming babies.

After arriving in San Juan, I checked into El Convento Hotel located in Old San Juan. While there was no air conditioning, my room had really tall windows which allowed available breezes to cool the space. During my stay in San Juan, I did a number of things that were fairly brave for a self-described shy introverted guy who only knew a few words of Spanish. For instance, I caught a "publico" and traveled from San Juan to the city of Ponce. Publicos were private cars that traveled between points identified on the respective car windshields. For instance, the publico that I took from Old San Juan to Ponce had a posted sign reading, "San Juan a Ponce". While I can't remember how or where I found the information regarding publicos, I actually got into the backseat of a San Juan a Ponce vehicle and kind of hunkered down as the driver made multiple stops while picking up and dropping off passengers along the way.

Things were going very well for me during the earlier leg of the trip. The driver had the radio on and there was a content stream of talk and music which I had no clue as to what was being said or sung. No matter. Everyone else was smiling, nodding and making commentary to each other, everyone else except me. I was sitting there with a stony face because I felt that I was in way over my head insofar as cultural and linguistic immersion was concerned.

After and hour or so of this, a twenty-something year old young man turned to me and said something that, by inflection, sounded like a question in Spanish. Coincidentally, I was seated in the middle of the back seat when this occurred. I responded in English that I did not speak Spanish and did not understand what he had said. Well, everyone including the driver suddenly turned to me and stared, mouths agape as if they were thinking, oh, my God! This guy is not Puerto Rican! Why is he in this vehicle with the rest of us? Apparently, at the time, mainland tourists did not hang out in publicos with the native population.

Caribbean Capers

As I recall, my personal safety was not a concern. Instead, of most concern to me was the embarrassment that I could neither speak, nor understand the language of the people of a land in which I was a visitor/guest/interloper. Even so, I refused to be deterred by my ignorance. Using San Juan as my base, I took a ferry trip to Fajardo and a public bus to Mayaguez. I can't remember how I got to Luquillo and El Yunque, the tropical rainforest. A city bus provided transportation to Santurce and Rio Piedras, where I walked the grounds of the university. The only memorable thing about the food was that I had dinner in the restaurant of one of the beachside hotels and ordered something that I think was called a pineapple surprise. In fact, I experienced two surprises. The first was that the chicken-rice-pineapple combination was served in a hollowed out pineapple wrapped in purple cellophane and the second was that I had a very bad case of heartburn during and after eating. Beware of purple cellophane!

The St. Thomas portion of the trip was not at all problematic. Everyone that I met spoke English at least as well as I did although with a rhythm that I could not match. Cementing this conclusion was my encounter with a local, David Chinnery, one afternoon in the bar of my hotel, the Gate Hotel, Charlotte Amalie. We talked and talked and drank and drank until the topic of food came up. More specifically, David brought up the term souse, an island treat he said. Turned out that island souse was the same thing that we called hog head cheese back home in Gainesville, Florida. David knew of an eating establishment, he said, that had great souse. Because my belly was crying out, "Feed me! Feed me!" I was more than ready for a little gastronomic adventure. Luckily, we were able to walk to the souse place. While my memory is a little foggy about most details of the meal, two other things still stand out in sharp relief. One is that the souse with beets was not disappointing. The other is that of several cockroaches climbing on the walls while I was eating, a fact which did not seem to disturb me in the least. In all likelihood, copious intake of rum before the souse had lowered my sense of propriety and hygiene.

Again, details are sketchy at best but David mentioned his wife, mother, and son with whom he lived. He wanted to know whether I wanted to meet them.

My positive response led to a short walk to the family home. Minutes later, we were seated in the backyard drinking Remy Martin cognac with Pepsi Cola chasers. Like David, the family was warm, welcoming, and very hospitable.

The Gate Hotel was located up a hill from the harbor area and a restaurant called Sparky's, I think. Over the days of my visit to St. Thomas, I spent quite a few hours sitting on the restaurant deck, eating, drinking, and watching movement in the harbor. Now this was the life!

As a self-described introvert, my lack of hesitancy in taking a risk in meeting and hanging out with people like David and his family and my Spanish-language-challenge adventure with fellow passengers in the publico a few days earlier present contradictions that could use an explanation. While the former was most likely influenced by booze, the latter experience was totally boozeless. Hmm!

Over several years after the Puerto Rico and St. Thomas, Virgin Islands trip, I journeyed to Barbados and Antigua; Jamaica; St.

Croix; Bonaire; Trinidad and Tobago; Haiti; Grenada; Martinique; and Guadaloupe. Some memories of those experiences are far more deeply embedded in my mind than are others. Bonaire, for example, one of the three so-called A, B, C islands of the Leeward Antilles (Aruba, Bonaire, Curacao) remains near the top of the list.

Never ever having been a competent swimmer, I was elated to read beforehand that reef fish could be observed just a few feet from the water's edge even in depths of only 2 or 3 feet. Boy, was the book correct! I spent many hours snorkeling near the beach and had my first encounters with parrot fish among others. Parrot fish were the largest multi-colored species that I could see so near the beach. When I wasn't in the water, I would take long walks along the road bordering the hotel, Hotel Bonaire, in case someone forgot what island they were on. During one of my walks, I came across an area in which there were many wild flamingos. I mean, there the flamingos were standing as if they were waiting for their "close-up" for some Hollywood production. The only downside at Hotel Bonaire occurred during an evening in which I decided that I was going to visit the casino. Problem. I was wearing sandals and the security man said uh, uh. He pointed to a nearby sign that clearly stated that sandals were not allowed inside the casino. Oh well, their loss. I had planned to spend heavily-all the way up to $10.

While in Barbados, there were two situations which darkly colored my days there. I think that the name of the hotel was the Blue Water Beach Hotel. On one of the nights, a group of musicians was scheduled to entertain after dinner. This was a small hotel where the dining room also served as the entertainment space. During set-up time in which sound equipment was being installed, tested, etc. I chose a table with only three other chairs and sat as unobtrusively as I could. Next thing that I remember, the white manager was yelling at me that I could not sit in the seat that I had chosen. He spoke in such a loud disrespectful tone that I felt like I was the dishwasher who had forgotten his job and now was trying to hang out with the paying guests. There were no signs or anything that suggested that there were unoccupied tables at which one was not allowed to sit. The second event took place in the bar where I had gone to have a drink and perhaps meet some of the similarly thirsty folks. Towards one end of the bar stood a small group of people, males and females. They formed a kind of semi-circle in relation to the bar. It seemed that some of the chatters were biracial or mulattos or some such mixture. They occupied that space for quite some time and it was obvious that they were satisfied with the mix of their group and were not welcoming to outsiders. Not being encumbered by facts, I got the very strong impression that other folks in the bar were of similar feelings, strangers not welcome. I have described these emotions to others after getting back stateside and had my impressions confirmed. A significant number of Bajans were not friendly. Despite what some stateside "Bajans" have tried to tell me, Barbados remains firmly on my Do-Not-Go-There-Again list. Decades later, Barbados remains on that list, right up there with Saudi Arabia.

Access to the beach required a walk across a highway then several more steps to beautiful white sands, then the surf. The surf could get pretty rough. On another day, I took an open-sided bus into Bridgetown. This was going to be another time of discovery for me until I realized that there was nothing to discover at the time. After walking around for a while, I took the bus back to the hotel/beach area.

Despite having made two separate trips to Jamaica, very little stands out in my mind. What does trouble me until this day is my distracted behavior while trying to dance with a lady whom I had met a few times at parties back in New York. I was depressed and mentally caught up in the stormy drama of my second marriage. I had managed to bring the whole sack full of crap with me. It wasn't until she said to me, "Gene, stop. It's o.k." or words to that effect, before she walked away. Never again have I seen that lady to offer an apology.

Nothing else in the all-inclusive Negril Beach Village could shake me from my depression.

Another memory of Jamaica which stands out was an occasion where I had borrowed a bicycle from the hotel. I wanted to explore the areas nearby. Finding a small sandy access road that connected the highway (where hotel was) to the beach, I decided to walk the bike to the beach. While standing in an isolated area, checking out sand and surf, I saw a guy approaching on a bicycle. As he got nearer, I noticed that his skin color was about the same as a cup of instant coffee without milk. The closer he came, the more I could see of his blood-red eyes and weird leer or grin. While I don't recall wetting my shorts due to this encounter, I felt very threatened. Did he have a weapon? Was he going to demand my wallet before physically assaulting me? Fortunately, none of my fears were realized. I believed that he was trying to sell me ganja which would have explained his blood-shot eyes, nearly incoherent language, and weird grin. After a few minutes he went on his way and I, somewhat shakily, went on mine. WHEW!

My trip to Trinidad and Tobago was framed by pre-trip mistakes, my mistakes.

First, I booked the trip for September, a month that falls during the time of the year which tends to have the highest level of tropical storms and hurricanes in the Caribbean and U.S. Gulf coastal states. Secondly, I thought that I had booked a room in a Port of Spain Hilton Hotel. The hotel staff could find no reservation for me at that location nor did I have any confirmation or other proof. To make matters even worse, there was no room in the inn. The place was solidly booked. When I asked for suggestions someone at the desk mentioned a less popular and more remote hotel a fair distance from the center of Port of Spain. A telephone call was made and that is how I came to spend a few rainy days near the outskirts of Port of Spain. I remember that the hotel floor was linoleum, not carpet, and that the heavy rainfall and humidity were so high that I could see my bare footprints when I walked across the floor. The only food that I remember was roti. I was told that this stew-like dish eaten with Indian-style flat bread was a typical dish of Trinidad.

On Tobago, I spent a few days at a guesthouse. I was awakened during the night because I thought that I was having a nightmare in which the building moved. During breakfast the next morning, everyone was talking about the earthquake that occurred during the night. It seemed that my bed along with the building had indeed moved, the results of an earthquake that took place near Venezuela. While there was little else memorable that happened during my Trinidad and Tobago trip, the earthquake provided me with another story that I could tell to anyone who had the patience to listen.

My Caribbean Capers were off to a good start. But I had more tales to collect and tell about other Caribbean islands still to be visited.

FRIENDS

No, this story is not about the popular television show of the same name, even though New York City was pivotal in both the fictional versions and this story about real people. The real people, in this case, are the folks that I have felt closest to, some over a period of more than 55 years. I have variously referred to many of those people as my posse, my group, my friends. Please note the possessive descriptors.

This trip down nostalgia lane started during a weekend in which I seemed on the verge of losing it. I was depressed and angry over the continuing side effects that I was experiencing because of daily, Monday through Friday, pelvic radiation therapy treatments for advanced prostate cancer. The side effects manifested as problems of The Three B's-bladder, bowel, and bleeding. Because of bladder inflammation from the radiation, I was having to go to the bathroom about every hour, both night and day. Worst of all, the urgency was such that I had a window of about 60 seconds to get to the bathroom from wherever I was standing or sitting when the urge struck. Simultaneously, compounding the urinary problems, there was the involuntary leakage of fecal content if I did not sit on the commode immediately. YUCK!

During one weekend, I had to change my underwear 5 times because I had not effectively managed the 60-second rule. Rarely had my body been so autonomous, especially while I was stone cold sober. Because I was so into my self-pity, I neither wanted to speak with nor otherwise correspond with any other human beings, be they family or friends or foe. My mind-state and corresponding behavior at the time is only available to folks who live alone, in my opinion. Only folks living in singular isolation can achieve this level of self-indulgence. I was slowly approaching the, "Oh, why me?" stage of my illness.

So, into this maelstrom of emotions and symptoms and isolation came an email and a telephone call from a New York friend, Dorothy Brooks Vock. She repeated both the next day, Sunday. By Monday, I was feeling a bit better emotionally, even though nothing had changed regarding the 3-B's. With this improvement in my emotional status, I re-read Dorothy's emails and replayed the telephone messages. I was especially struck by the sentiments that she expressed in the second email. It opened with a kind of threat that said that I was not going to get rid of her so easily by remaining incommunicado. Furthermore, she added that she and others loved me and were concerned about my well-being. After another couple of sentences, she ended with the notation, BBFF. While I was observant enough to know what the BFF ending meant, BBFF completely threw me. The mystery was solved a few hours later during my telephone call to Dorothy, when she informed me that BBFF meant best black friend forever. I couldn't stop chuckling. The messaging, the care, the concern, the love, and the almost 60-year duration of our friendship all nearly reduced me to tears. I decided that day that I would try to write a story that would attempt to describe my involvement in the social group, The Coffee Breakers, which Dorothy started back around 1957 or so. I also wanted to describe some of the other significant friendships that developed over the years that were so important to my sense of well-being and fun.

Friends

I think I need to tell you a little about my childhood, teenage and young adult years to enable you to see how the path that led to my making and keeping friends could have easily taken me to a very different and much darker place. A good memory has made much of what I experienced over the years, the facts and the feelings, readily accessible to me. Moreover, I have visited, assessed and re-assessed the past with regularity.

I grew up, essentially, as a bit of a loner and introvert. I read lots of comic books, old National Geographic magazines and any other book or magazine that I could get my hands on. Reading was my favorite pastime during my preteen and early teen years. Along with reading, I enjoyed bike riding and experimenting with my chemistry set or microscope set that my parents gave me, one each on successive Christmases around age 12 or 13. Indeed, I chased Chris Burroughs, classmate and neighbor, away from our house on a number of occasions after he had overstayed his welcome and fallen asleep on our back porch. Putting a test tube of freshly generated hydrogen sulfide gas under Chris' nose worked every time. Only one whiff did the trick.

While I did play with other kids in the neighborhood occasionally, I could only do so with my mother's permission. On more than one occasion, she used a switch on me because I had sneaked across the street to play with one or more of the Williams children without her permission. Gertrude Williams and I were about the same age and were classmates from first grade thru 12th grade graduation. One of Ma's favorite rejoinders while denying me permission to go some place was, "No. This yard is plenty big enough for you". At other times, my mother's message to me, invariably, was that I was lazy and would never amount to anything. A positive message from either parent regarding anything that I did was non-existent. This despite report cards filled with A's and a few B's over the years, the responses that I felt were silence and disinterest.

By the time that my teenage years rolled around, I had absorbed my mother's messaging and was angry often regarding her behavior and my father's distance and indifference. As a result, I usually felt like and behaved like an angry, sullen, withdrawn, fear-ridden lonely mess while at home. Unloved and unwanted were words that fit my feelings perfectly. For a while, I tried to hide or disappear. To accomplish this, I wore an army surplus hat with turned-down brim that pretty much concealed my face from view. Also during my early teenage years, I spoke to my parents only when I had no choice.

I was not allowed to express any opinion that differed from whatever negative conclusions that my mother had reached about me. Almost always, it was about some chore that I was accused of not having done (usually pretty accurate) or having done poorly in my mother's eyes. I must admit that I hated doing chores because there was no reward at all. No thank you. No job well done. Ma's standards for each chore were pretty high. My silent resistance was also pretty high. Anyone would have been hard-pressed to ever observe any overt signs of affection or approval from either parent.

On the other hand, it was also true that there was always something to eat in our house. Our clothes were always clean and neatly ironed. The house was always clean and neat. I don't ever recall telling either parent about some school project for which I needed a small amount of money and was denied same. There was almost always a Christmas tree with a present for my older sister and me while birthdays were never recognized.

Friends

By contrast, my life at school was nearly the opposite of my experiences at home. Nearly all of my teachers saw me as a model student because of my grades and class behavior. While in fourth grade, our principal, Mr. Cook, saw me walking towards him in the hallway during an authorized break. He smiled and said, "Here comes the Little Professor." My seventh grade social studies teacher even spent several minutes one day lecturing the rest of the class on why they should be more like me. I found this highly embarrassing and wanted to dig a deep hole and hide. Amazingly, I was never picked on by my classmates for this kind of attention. If the truth be told, I enjoyed the attention and I enjoyed school immensely. In school, I was valued, praised, and readily accepted by both my teachers and classmates. At home, I was tolerated at best and often scolded for being lazy. There was an on-going conflict with my mother. My agenda nearly always differed from hers. Of course, she always had the upper hand.

One night when I was about 15, the same struggle and condemnations occurred because I did not start washing dishes soon enough. For me, this was a slam too far. After my parents had retired and both of them were in bed and the room darkened, I stormed into their bedroom, tears streaming down my face and snot running from my nose. I had silently worked myself into a tear-filled rage which exploded at the foot of their bed. I told them both that I was tired of their criticisms and put-downs and that they never had anything positive to say to me. Many other words tumbled out of my mouth that night. I unloaded years of anger, pain and hurt. This was such a radical change in my behavior that I think that I actually frightened them both. I do not know whether they were aware of the movie, "The Bad Seed". However, the pent up emotions that suddenly broke through the dam could not have been a pretty sight to see and may not have portended well for the future.

But my breakdown served its purpose. The nagging put-downs stopped and I became far more responsible by doing chores without being told, both inside the house and in my father's automobile repair shop later on. Still, as a teenager, I felt incredibly lonely and out of place, at home. I felt as if I was a total stranger and neither of the two parents were my real parents.

As a preteen, on Saturday mornings, I would sneak into the house and listen to radio broadcasts of the Los Angeles Symphony's youth concerts. Because I was stealing time from doing my chores, these were acts of illicit learning and appreciation. Listening to these concerts started my love of classical music.

In seventh grade, I asked for permission to take piano lessons. There was an old upright piano in the living room which my older sister, Margaret, had used while she took lessons for a couple of years. Parental permission was granted and I began taking lessons from my seventh grade homeroom teacher, Ms. Louise Hill. Unfortunately, my ambition far exceeded my talents and patience with piano exercises. I quit after only five lessons. After I quit, Ms. Hill gave an angry lecture during one of our classes in which she berated individuals who had potentials but threw away opportunities for development of latent talent. For some reason, while she did not call me by name, she focused her gaze on me. Now, why would she be singling me out? The urge to play music continued even after my failed attempt to master the piano by my fifth lesson. By eighth grade, I decided that I wanted to join the high school band which had been organized only the year before.

Friends

I sought and gained parental permission. The band director assigned the mellophone (E flat horn) to me, the same instrument that my older cousin, Willie Coleman, played in the band. AAAhhhh! This was it! While my mother discouraged me from "making all that noise" by rehearsing at home, class schedules for band members were altered so that music lessons with the band director replaced mandatory physical education classes. YES! I hated P.E.!

Learning to read music was no problem for me. For the first couple of years in the band, I would do well in ensemble work but would nearly fall apart with anxiety when a solo passage was required of me. My self confidence sucked big time. Eventually, I gained enough confidence that I was named first horn player. The band was a full-school-year activity with marching band rehearsals and performances during football season and rehearsals and performances during "concert" season. Concert season was the cat's meow as far as I was concerned. We got to play music by some really serious folks, Brahms, von Suppe, Saint-Saens, Dvorak, among others. Annually, we competed in the Florida High School Bands Festival (blacks only) held in various cities of the state. We also played concerts at various black churches in and around Gainesville in addition to an annual concert in our high school's auditorium. Invariably, after these gigs, neighbors and fellow-band members Chester Williams, Claretha Jenkins, and I would walk together (dressed in our blue and gold band uniforms) from Lincoln High School in Northwest Gainesville back to our respective homes in the Porters Neighborhood of Southwest Gainesville. Our conversations were always without rancor even though I no longer have a clue as to what we talked about. I dug it all.

Tales of a Black Sojourner

Before graduating from Lincoln High, I applied to and was accepted by the Xavier University College of Pharmacy in New Orleans Louisiana. During my four years there, I made a few friends, some of whom were college of pharmacy classmates. Two of my nasty-cussing, embarrassingly loud classmates were George Danner of Orlando and Morgan Richard of St. Petersburg. Another Floridian and pharmacy student was Nat Willis of Orlando. He was noted for pretty much the same behavior as the other two Floridians. Some of the other dorm dwellers who knew us all swore that I could not possibly be a Floridian because I was too quiet and didn't cuss. (I have since made up for that deficiency.) Unfortunately, these friendships had fairly short expiry dates post-graduation. Then, there was Moses Rabb, a liberal arts major from Rock Hill, S.C. Moses and I were about the same age and both members of the class of 1956. He was Catholic while I was (at the time) Baptist. Many of the conversations between Moses and me were about religion and philosophy, as I recall. These were topics about which I knew little or nothing. So convincing were Moses' beliefs and knowledge regarding Catholic Church history and teachings that I converted to Catholicism in my junior year. Moses was my godfather/sponsor during the baptismal ceremony. We lost touch after graduation but reconnected many years later after accidentally meeting him and another classmate, Reginald Matthews, in New York City's Times Square one day. Of course, I must now use the term doctor when I refer to either Moses or his wife, Gael. They both earned Ph.D.'s in Psychology. He specialized in clinical psychology and she in social psychology. We continue to correspond periodically. I even got the couple to do a presentation at one of our maternal family gatherings in Hardeeville S.C. Moses has a consultancy, Interventions Unlimited. The doctors Rabb live in Columbia S.C. with their daughter.

Friends

Upon graduating from Xavier in 1956, I temporarily returned to Gainesville with my B.S. degree in hand. Opportunities in Gainesville for a black pharmacy graduate were non-existent. Besides which, my hatred for both New Orleans and Gainesville were pretty high. Not knowing anything better to do, I called my sister, Margaret, and her then husband, Earnest, to see whether they would permit me to stay with them in East Orange, New Jersey until I could find a job in pharmacy. With their consent, using cash prize award money that I received at graduation, I took a bus from Gainesville to Newark New Jersey.

After about three weeks and zero successes in New Jersey, I received a fateful telephone call from my father's aunt, Aunt Nan. In her inimitable fashion, Aunt Nan informed me that if one were to do anything with one's life, one did not do such in New Jersey, one did it in New York. So, I was ordered to move from East Orange to share Aunt Nan's Harlem five room apartment on St. Nicholas Avenue. As Aunt Nan predicted, I soon found a job which lasted about two months.

The end came when my boss, Stanley Drucker, announced that he was closing the pharmacy for a 2 week vacation starting the following Monday. He further informed me that because I had not worked in the pharmacy long enough to earn a vacation, I would essentially be on an unpaid leave for the duration of the store's closure. As was proprietor, Stanley Drucker's custom during the two months that I worked for him, he lectured me for several moments duration every Saturday night before handing me the remnants of my $35 per week paycheck for a 6-day work-week. The lectures were all about my incompetence and failures to measure up to his changing expectations. He even criticized the slowness of my Southern speech. It should be pointed out that Stanley Drucker was the sole owner of Drucker's Pharmacy, a

Jewish-owned operation in the heart of a black neighborhood in the Bedford-Stuyvesant area of Brooklyn. Doc, as the people of the neighborhood called him, pushed the envelope of misrepresentation. He was very good at shaping his message of tolerance and equality with his black customers while he sought to repeatedly undermine my self-confidence. In that he was quite successful. He had me place my Xavier degree in a prominent shelf above the cash register and would not so subtly point to it and tell a lie to his customers about how glad he was to have hired me.

Drucker was more than a master manipulator. My sense of failure was such that I knew that he was absolutely correct in his assessment of my job performance. Here, I had been successful in college. Class president in my junior and senior years. Honor rolls in all but my sophomore year when a disruptive roommate and physics nearly did me in. In my senior year, I worked part-time mopping/waxing floors in the university's cafeteria. I was quasi-assistant editor of our class yearbook, working on layouts and corresponding texts, drawings, and photographs while carrying the equivalent of 22/23 semester hours. Oh, I also worked several hours on Sundays at Boutte's Pharmacy on Galvez Street in New Orleans.

While I had been successful in school, I was obviously failing in life. My sense of failure was so profound that I had begun to seriously consider suicide. The bridges over the East River were becoming more and more attractive as places from which I could end my misery. Now, where had I been lectured to before regarding my failures to measure up to the expectations of others? Why, the house in which I grew up. Ma's predictions were certainly coming true. Why, I couldn't even successfully hold down a $35 per week job in a field in which I had spent four years of preparation. Worst of all, there was no one that I felt comfortable with while talking about my predicament.

Until this day, it is with some pride that I report that on the day that Stanley Drucker opened his pharmacy post-vacation, I called and told him that I would not be coming to work anymore because I had already started on another job as a pharmacist (unlicensed) with a pharmaceutical manufacturer in Long Island City. I never set foot in Drucker's Pharmacy again, not even to pick up my diploma. Good riddance, Drucker, you ------.!

While on the subway returning from my Long Island City job to my aunt's apartment one afternoon, I looked up from whatever had been occupying my attention and there sat one of my Xavier classmates, Pat Ferguson. It was an enthusiastic and joyful reunion. She informed me that she was sharing an apartment with another classmate, Nina Heyward. In the same Harlem building, there was another apartment shared by Mrs. Mary Brooks and her daughter, Dorothy. Dorothy had spent one semester at Xavier before returning to New York and enrolling at New York University. Also sharing the apartment was another Xavierite who had finished the year before my class, the class of 1956. Lo and behold, it was Marva Parks, a New Orleans native.

While I don't remember the order in which things unfolded subsequently, major changes occurred which pretty much changed my then fledgling life in New York. One was the formation of a group by Dorothy that would partake of various cultural and entertainment events happening in New York City. The first order of business after the group formed was a discussion of the book, Black Bourgeoisie. The book was written by black sociologist, E. Franklin Frazier. The group chose as its name, The Coffee

Breakers. For some reason, I missed the initial meeting and book discussion. Subsequent meetings, however, were attended by a group of about ten young black males and females mainly from the segregated South. Except for Dorothy and one other person in the group, all of us had graduated from historically black colleges and universities located in the South. Jimmy Galloway was the other exception. He held an undergraduate degree from Lincoln University in Pennsylvania and was completing a masters in business at New York University. Moreover, he was from Roxboro Massachusetts, not exactly rebel territory. Jimmy was an outlier in a couple of other ways: He was the tallest person in the group at around 6'1" or so, light skinned, freckles (I think), and loved to debate topical issues. With his horned rim glasses and neat business attire, he had already affected the look of success. Jimmy often bragged about Lincoln University and its distinguished alumni including former Supreme Court Justice, Thurgood Marshall. He was also very proud of his fraternal affiliation as a "Q", Omega Psi Phi fraternity. We lost track of Jimmy after he earned his masters degree and returned to the Boston area. Dorothy left New York in 1958 to become a guide at the Brussels World Fair. Her fluency in French and interest in French culture probably made the hiring decision a no-brainer. Also in her favor was her experience working as a guide at the United Nations headquarters in New York City.

For a while, Jimmy and Leo Sam, another charter-member of The Coffee Breakers, were roommates who shared an apartment on West 87th Street in Manhattan. Leo Sam was from Beaumont Texas and graduated from Xavier University in 1952, a semester before I arrived on campus. According to Leo, one of his personal goals was to work in Africa. He left New York and our group somewhere around 1959 or 1960. He became director of Catholic Relief Services in Senegal first, then Morocco, after which came Holland. Later, at some point in his various incarnations in Europe and the U.S., he became an expert in investment strategies and later, landed positions as advisor to university presidents. I can't remember how or when I reconnected with Leo after all of his stellar international successes. However, I am happy to report that he appears to have retained a sense of humility, curiosity, and humor. He has attended a couple of celebrations at my house in Gainesville. He and my younger sister, Mildred, can and do put on quite a show, especially around topics of golden-age marriages, pre-nups, and who is going to take care of whom if and when they marry.

Frank and Lynette Hamilton are friends of Leo and accompanied him when he attended our 2013 Memorial Day celebration in Gainesville. Leo and the Hamiltons live in the Tallahassee area. Lynette is a retired biology professor and Frank is a retired research chemist and both were staffers at Florida A. and M. University. Despite their academic and research achievements (Ph.D,'s each) there is a sense that each of them place far more importance on being genuine, humble, but highly intelligent and very social human beings. If Leo is not careful, my family is going to steal the Hamiltons from him.

During the late fifties or so, living on the same block of West 87th Street as Jimmy Galloway and Leo were Martha Brown and her brother, Jonathan Brown. These two were graduates of Virginia State University. Martha and Leo first met each other while enrolled in the same class at N.Y.U.'s school of business. At the same time, Jonathan was working on a master's degree in accountancy at the same school. Jimmy, Leo, Martha, and Jonathan all worked at full-time jobs while pursuing graduate degrees. After getting his masters degree, Jonathan took a job with U.S.A.I.D. and worked in East Africa for a couple of years. Martha finished her masters at N.Y.U. and worked as an educator and held other administrative posts with the New York City Board of Education.

Ruth Jackson, native Virginian, good friend of Martha, and also a graduate of Virginia State University earned her masters degree in social work from Columbia University. She was an addition to the membership roster of the Coffee Breakers. She accompanied Martha, Leo, and Jonathan to Gainesville when I held my open house and belated birthday party in October of 2010. (Birthday, August 1st.) Coincidentally, during my open house/belated birthday celebration, in addition to family, my guests consisted of classmates from elementary school (we started out in first grade together), high school, Xavier, New York, and post-Saudi Arabia periods. Added were a few friends of relatives, especially Michelle and Reno. She, a licensed advanced nurse practitioner from Connecticut and he, a civil engineer from New Jersey. Reno and Michelle are a couple who, while visiting, spent several minutes trying to convince me that I should begin writing stories about my life experiences. Blame them, among others, if you are so bored that you stop reading before you get to the end of this story. Besides Michelle and Reno being two bright and perceptive people, Reno had this right brain, left brain dichotomy thing going on. In addition to being an analytical kind of guy, he could also reel off facts about history, recite poetry and passages from literary works with the greatest of ease. Man, he is weird! (But also very impressive).

Also part of The Coffee Breakers for a while was Marva Parks. Marva was a math major at Xavier while on an academic scholarship. She maintained her scholarship by earning only one B during her four years at the university. An A in every other class led to her graduating Magna Cum Laude in 1955. She was awarded a fellowship to pursue a master's degree at N.Y.U. After receiving the masters and while pursuing a Ph.D. in math, Marva taught calculus and differential equations to students of New York's Queens College. At Xavier, I think many a dude was intimidated by Marva's height (around 5'10" or so) and/or brain. I do believe that everyone on Xavier's campus knew who she was. Some in our ranks dreaded finding out that she would be a fellow student in any of our classes because she would set the bar so high. Despite her smarts, Marva had a great sense of humor and liked to party right along with the rest of us. For a while, Marva and I became occasional ice skating partners, usually trying our luck at Sky Rink above New York City's Madison Square Garden. Two southerners trying to learn to ice skate for the very first time must have been quite a sight to see.

I was quite shocked one night when Marva told me that she was leaving New York. My shock was intensified when she told me that not only was she leaving New York, she was also getting married. Pouring on more shock, she said that she was marrying her classmate, Roland Pattillo. Roland Pattillo? But, but how can that be? The three of us had been active in student government at the same time at Xavier and I had never sensed any kind of spark between them. Not only that, campus gossip had linked Roland with at least one other young lady on campus. (Xavier's total enrollment at the time was only 1200 students, including grad students.) Not too long after that, Marva did indeed leave New York and married Roland who had earned his M.D. degree from Washington University in St. Louis. From time to time, I would hear about Marva and her growing family (She and Roland stopped at 5 kids) through our mutual friend, Dorothy. Over the years, Marva has had incarnations as mother, grandmother, small business owner, faculty member at Marquette University in Milwaukee Wisconsin, and world traveler. We re-established contact many years ago while I was living and working in Chicago and Marva and her family were living in Milwaukee Wisconsin where Roland was on the faculty at the Medical College of Wisconsin. Marva's range of interests has only grown over time. Oh, I nearly forgot. Marva is also a trained pianist and voracious reader. I know these things as facts because while I was on a brief visit to Milwaukee, she sat down at her piano and played one of my favorite compositions, Malaguena by Cuban composer, Ernesto Lecuona.

All stateside friendships were put on hold while I pursued a job opportunity in Saudi Arabia. The work environment for me as Associate Director of Pharmacy at Rush-Presbyterian Medical Center (now Rush Medical Center) Chicago, had become intolerably toxic. Issues of narcissism and ego-mania at the top of the departmental organizational structure were more than I cared to tolerate. During the four years in which I was employed at Rush, I made no friends at all even among the couple of other black pharmacists working there at the time. With nearly 120 employees in the department, opportunities for skullduggery and back-stabbing did not go unused. I couldn't wait to bid goodbye to that whole scene. So, in September of 1987, I flew from Chicago via New York to Riyadh Saudi Arabia to assume the position of Director of Pharmacy at the King Khaled Eye Specialist Hospital. More details about that journey in another story. I returned to Gainesville in January of 1989 after visiting Thailand, Hong Kong, Malaysia, Singapore, and Australia. On return to Gainesville, I attempted to re-establish ties with classmates from high school and one fellow student from Xavier who had relocated to Gainesville. It was very difficult. I got the feeling that I was seen as some kind of interloper, known by name and face yet unfamiliar nevertheless. After a year or so of "efforting", I threw in the towel. No matter, I decided that I would settle in Gainesville. Got a job, bought a car (used) and a house. Even joined the United Church of Gainesville, a very liberal congregation where I made a couple of friends, the duration of such friendships lasting about 4 or 5 years before weirdness set in. Was invited to join a men's group which I readily accepted. If memory serves me correctly, the group lasted for nearly 2 years before it collapsed.

The United Church had only four or five blacks in its congregation and there were times when I felt really uncomfortable and out of place. However, from the men's group, John Korb and I continued to keep in touch. After his sister, Mitzi, relocated to Gainesville from California, each of us became regular attendees at dinners or parties in our respective homes. While attending black churches I experienced another kind of discomfort. The focus on Jesus, being born again, and the exceptionalism of Christianity to the exclusion of all other faiths simply did not sit well with me. After all, I had personally experienced the devotion of adherents of other faiths including Buddhists, Moslems, and Hindus within their cultural framework. Why would a loving and just God punish this sincerity of devotion and condemn huge swaths of the global population to the eternal pits of hell? It made no sense to me then and makes no sense to me now. Despite my rejection of some Christian teachings, I truly love black gospel music, not so much for the lyrics but for the spirit and rhythms embodied in the music. It doesn't take too much to get my feet tapping, even hand-clapping. I continue to draw a line when other congregants stand and sing and shout. Way too much attention for me.

One of the other things that I started doing after getting settled into my Gainesville house was holding celebrations of various types in my home. Initially, it was all about family - parent's birthdays, Christmas, etc. Then, slowly, I started inviting a few people from the past to join family members. After retiring from full-time employment with the State of Florida in 1999, I moved the locus of some of the celebrations to Hilton Head S.C. I even started writing a newsletter centered around family gatherings on Hilton Head, a city in the Low Country of South Carolina about 35 or 40 minutes from the site of my maternal grandmother's farm and the place in which my mother and her siblings were born. On at least three occasions, a couple of Xavier classmates actually joined members of my family during these get-togethers. An invitation also went out to some of the members of the original Coffee Breakers with whom I had re-established contact.

One of the other persons with whom I re-established contact after graduation was Reginald Matthews. At some point in 1956 or 1957 while walking to Harlem's St. Charles Borromeo Catholic Church one Sunday morning to attend mass, I realized that I was staring into the face of Reginald Matthews, a Xavier classmate. Reginald was a native of Panama and had begun a masters program in biology at St. John's University in the New York City Borough of Queens. We exchanged telephone numbers and promised to keep in touch.

Promises were kept. One day while on duty as a pharmacist at Lenox Hill Hospital in Manhattan (my first job as a registered pharmacist in New York), one of my co-workers told me that there was a nurse at the window who wanted to talk to me. As I approached the window, I saw this tall willowy young lady dressed in white scrubs. She introduced herself as Anne Lawson, a "friend" of Reginald Matthews. Anne was a volunteer registered nurse working in the nursery at Lenox Hill. She further informed me that for her regular gig, she worked as a head nurse in one of the operating rooms of New York Hospital. Anne earned her B.S. degree in nursing from Hampton Institute in Virginia (now Hampton University). Anne and Reginald attended a number of our parties and other group activities in New York.

Friends

In 1958, I moved into my fifth floor, walk-up studio apartment in a building dubbed by its owners as the Garden of Eden. It was located on East 4th Street between 1st and 2nd Avenues. A dark-green canopy over the sidewalk announced that you had indeed reached the infamous building in which the lobby had a full wall-sized mural containing representations of Adam, Eve, appropriately placed leaves, all in the presence of a peacock and a cock-eyed lion. It continues to be my opinion that the muralist was high on something while doing the job and got his/her perspective a bit askew. The apartment was smack dab in the heart of the East Village during the time in which struggling artists and artist-wannabes, and writers were moving east from the West Village because rents were far more affordable. My newly acquired bachelor pad was probably no more than about 200 square feet including the kitchen and bathroom areas. The sole closet was only about 4 foot wide but contained all of my clothes that couldn't be folded into a make-shift desk/bookcase/chest unit.

In some ways, this tiny personal space represented an escape from Aunt Nan's verbal abuse that worsened after I notified her of my intent to move. I was then truly independent of the authority of older persons for the first time in my life. And boy! Did I try my best to thoroughly enjoy this newly-found freedom, especially on weekends. Practitioners from the Beat Generation (a.k.a. Beatniks) set the tone for pseudo-bohemians as I was trying to become, but only on weekends. For me however, work-days at Lenox Hill saw me trying my best to be an exemplary staff pharmacist and a couple of years later, pharmacy section supervisor. After all, I was the first black pharmacist hired at Lenox Hill Hospital. I know this because my boss, Robert Bogash, kept reminding me of his benevolence in that he gave me this chance.

During this time I also discovered the pleasures of booze. I even had a favorite liquor store a block west of my apartment building. I do believe that, over time, I purchased nearly every kind of wine that existed in the store. This propensity lead to occasional hangovers, some of which lasted into Monday morning. But hey, I was trying my darnedest to mimic the behavior of the really famous and highly talented dudes of the Beat Generation like Jack Kerouac. Unfortunately, these similarities existed only in my head in that I had no artistic talents but tried faking it on weekends.

Despite this admission however, my next door neighbor seemed to think that I had potential. Her name was Gloria C. Oden. She was a law school graduate from Howard University in Washington D.C. but decided after obtaining her degree that she did not like the law. (Go figure!) Instead, she was keen on staking out a path in literature. As I recall, she had had a poem published in one of the literary journals. Subsequently, she became associate editor of a small magazine called The Urbanite. I believe that one of her short stories was published in an issue of the magazine. Unfortunately, it folded after only 4 issues. Gloria was black but many of her male "friends" were white. Among those to whom she introduced me was a nationally known poet, Kenneth Rexroth and a famous novelist, Sloan Wilson. According to Wikipedia, Gloria was nominated for a Pulitzer Prize in 1979 for a volume of poetry that she had published. She retired as a full professor from University of Maryland, Baltimore County.

Across the hall from my little cell was Genevieve's apartment. Genevieve was a French war bride who married an American G.I. while he was stationed in France after World War II was over. She was quite striking with her clear blue eyes and blond hair. She had a deep interest in the occult. Among the courses that she took at the New School was a course in The Kabbalah. Please note that this occurred decades before the Kabbalah was discovered by Hollywood. Gloria, Genevieve, and I formed a friendship and modestly referred to ourselves as The Triumvirate of The Fifth Floor of 120 East Fourth Street. When I gave a party, the other two were automatically invited. When Genevieve was out and about in the Village it was not uncommon for her to ring up Gloria who would then ring my bell and tell me that we should meet Genevieve at some particular place invariably within walking distance. Spontaneity was the name of the game. One Sunday afternoon, the pattern repeated itself. This time, we had to meet Genevieve at The Egyptian Gardens, a restaurant with live entertainment in the form of a belly dancer. While sharing the ladies' room, Genevieve found out that the belly dancer was a Boston native and not from Cairo or Tangiers. At other times Gloria would call me with an invite to accompany her to visit one of her literary or artistic friends. That is how I came to experience my first taste of cachaca, a type of Brazilian firewater made from sugar cane. On this Sunday afternoon, we all sat on the writer's living room floor by candlelight and proceeded to talk, drink and get wasted on the host's supply.

With Gloria, there were two areas in which she felt that she was free to give me unsolicited advice. One was my flute playing and the other was my romantic life. Gloria would tell me, with some frequency, how soothing my music was. I had begun flute studies with a teacher who had earned quite a reputation among some musicians in New York. He was Henry Zlotnick, a flutist who had toured and played with John Phillip Sousa's band. Herbie Mann, jazz flutist extraordinaire in the late fifties and sixties, was very popular, especially with the ladies. I figured that if I learned to play the flute, then my chances with the ladies would be substantially improved. Hence, daily practices and playing pieces by Couperin, Rameau, Bach, etc. even a few jazz pieces like, "Take Five"

Tales of a Black Sojourner

On several occasions, Gloria tried to convince me that I would be far better off if I would, essentially, stop seeing the black women that I was involved with and find a white girlfriend who was on the same level as I was intellectually, hobbies, interests, etc. I felt that Gloria was projecting her own preferences onto me. Maybe she had a much higher opinion of me than I had of myself. Also, maybe she was far more impressed with my experimentations than I was. Besides studying/playing the flute, I also tried to learn how to paint (oils), ski (took multiple lessons but never moved beyond wedge turns and lower intermediate hills), draw (took community ed course but got only one remark from teacher during the term), and ice skating (didn't know that ankles could be as weak as mine). The travel bug had bitten me by then also.

Thanks to Gloria, I had a eureka moment that had to do with the thinness of the wall separating our small living spaces. My sleep sofa was on the opposite side of the wall as was her sleep couch. She came into my apartment one day and asked me if I had ever considered moving my sofa to the opposite wall, an exterior wall. She pointed out that the arrangement would provide a greater sense of privacy in that when I had guests, no one else arriving at the front door would be able to see the person or persons that I might be entertaining. It wasn't until I was in the process of moving furniture per her suggestion that the true basis of her input came to me. It had a lot more to do with her hearing sounds stemming from my sleep sofa, especially in the middle of the night. I was more than a bit embarrassed because until then, I had thought that my nocturnal activity was strictly private and shared only between me and the lady who was sharing my bed. Oh, the shame of having an audience!

Friends

During my five years at 120 East 4th Street, I held several parties, the invitees being mainly members of The Coffee Breakers plus my 2 neighbors. During my last party at that location, somewhere around 3 a.m., I looked around this tiny space and realized that everyone else had gone to sleep except me. There were bodies on the floor; bodies on the sofa and in every chair. There was no place left where I could sleep, no place else except the bathroom, that is. I got a pillow, a blanket, and put them into the bathtub. Before going to sleep in the tub, however, I wrote a note and hung it on the outside of the shower curtain. The sign read, "Please don't pee in the tub. I'm sleeping." Gene. I closed the curtain and managed to get a few hours of sleep. The last guest left somewhere near 7 a.m. on Sunday. House parties in various locations were one of the ways in which ties within the group were reinforced and maintained. During the last party mentioned above, one of the contributing factors towards guests not leaving earlier may have been a game that I created on the spot at the beginning of the evening. Because I had a piece of canvas board, some brushes, acrylics of various colors, and an easel, each guest was required to take 2 swigs from an alcoholic drink of their choice and add three strokes of paint to the canvas board. There were no restrictions as to the form of neither the strokes nor the colors. Alcohol-induced creativity was the order of the evening. Of course, some crazy background music added to the frenzy. The piece turned into an image that I dubbed "Schizo".

Alas, The Triumvirate of The Fifth Floor of 120 East Fourth Street began to crumble after about four years of so. Genevieve moved to parts unknown. Several months later, I moved into a high-rise Mitchell-Lama co-op in the Fort Green/Clinton Hills section of Brooklyn. Communications dried up after that. The Triumvirate was no more. But the Coffee Breakers were still together. Besides partying, one of the other influences that tended to support the continuation of the group were the Sunday dinners that Mrs.

Brooks made for about seven of us. While we were eating, she let us know that she had informally adopted us and wanted us to know about investments for the future including land ownership. Leo probably was in a better position to begin to earnestly listen to Mrs. Brooks. For others like me, it took much longer to capitalize on her freely shared wisdom.

Composition of the group kind of ebbed and flowed. Some core additions were Mae and Earl Johnson, sister and brother from Danville Virginia. She was a graduate of Kentucky State and he knew Martha and Jonathan Brown because each had attended and graduated from Virginia State. Also added to the group was Nora Harris, May's former roommate and fellow-graduate from Kentucky State University. Nora would become my favorite dancing partner.

Besides partying at the drop of a hat, the group's core engaged in a number of other activities. There was a ski trip to Catamount Mountain in Upstate New York one Sunday. About halfway to the mountain, the bus malfunctioned in some way that I can't remember. What I do remember is that we were stranded on the highway for some time until the malfunction was addressed. Worst of all, when we finally got to Catamount about 1 o'clock in the afternoon, the slopes were mainly ice. No one else in the group besides me had ever been on skis before. Not exactly an auspicious beginning for new skiers. We never went skiing as a group after that experience. Then there was the weekend in a house in High Falls New York. The kicker in this case was that there were no functioning falls. Drought or some other force had simply reduced the volume of water to puddles and trickles.

Friends

For a while, the group was integrated. Anne Kushner, and Linda (?) were friends of May Johnson while Myrt (?) was a friend of Earl. George Price was a special "friend" of May Johnson for a while. Then there was Bob Greenfield, my ski buddy and friend, or so I thought. For a while, I thought that Bob may have lost some of his "Jewishness" because of the volume of pork-laced collard greens that he ate at my kitchen table over several months, thanks to my sister Mildred's cooking. Bob was a Princeton graduate and sales person for a trophies/awards company. Finally, there appeared on the scene John Morrison, who decided, apparently, that he would not take no for an answer about May Johnson becoming his wife. John was Canadian and Caucasian. He was also incredibly accepting of the tongue lashing that May was more than capable of dishing out. While in their presence one night in their Stuyvesant Town apartment after they had married, I sat dumbfounded after she called him a white m----------r. Instead of a retaliatory response as I probably would have done, John responded with a smiley, "Oh, Mazie-Poo!". His restraint was incredible. John received his Ph.D. in Sociology, I think, then became an assistant professor at the University of Pennsylvania. She worked in student housing. Several of the group visited May and John while they were living in Philadelphia. We had a great time. It didn't seem to bother John that he was a bit of an outsider as far as the group was concerned. He remained his own man. A few years later John accepted a position as associate professor at Aurora University in Illinois. John and May bought a house in trendy liberal Oak Park Illinois while I worked in Chicago. Given May's willingness to freely express her opinion no matter who was listening, it was so hard for me to envision her as a faculty wife. Many years later I was shocked to hear that May had died from cancer. It was so unlike her to give in to anyone or anything (except for John and their daughter, maybe).

Further decimating the periphery of the old group was the death of Anne Lawson Matthews, Reginald Matthews' wife. Within two weeks, she had had a severe stroke and died of the consequences. Over the years, Anne and I had spent hours and hours on the telephone comparing notes regarding our respective parents. She and I were both born in August of 1934; our mothers and fathers were both the same ages. Her mother developed Alzheimer's dementia about 6 months after my mother did. Both of our fathers acted like butt-holes in the aftermath of the onset of dementia. At some point after an hour or so, either I would ask to speak to Reginald, my college classmate, or Anne would suggest that I speak to him. Reginald would swear that both Anne and I hated our fathers. It wasn't hate on either of our parts. It was just gratifying to talk to someone who was going through the same crap as I was. The conversation with Reginald would usually last for another half-hour or an hour. Besides the commonalities of our parent's situations, I obviously enjoyed talking to both of them because the focus was on totally different areas of our respective lives. Reginald came to Gainesville for my Open-House/Belated Birthday party weekend after Anne had passed away. Within a couple of years, Reginald developed urinary tract problems among other conditions and was dead within a couple of weeks of having taken ill. I am surprised how much I miss both of them. It's as if I have lost a part of myself. Reginald was my historian about all things Xavier University. He remembered persons and personalities about which I would really have to scour my brain to dig up images as to who the person or persons were on campus.

In 2001, I decided that I would reignite the travel bug that had been lying dormant for a while. Grand Circle Travel had a trip that fit snugly into my travel plans for the future, namely Portugal, Spain, and Tangiers Morocco. On the appointed departure date I flew into JFK and waited around for the evening flight via TAP Airlines with a connecting flight in Lisbon to Oporto (Porto) where the next leg of our trip was to begin. For one of the few times in my travel life, I became very confused once I landed in Lisbon. I saw no signs of any kind as to where in the airport complex I could find my connecting flight to Oporto. After wandering around and searching, I came upon a group of five people standing in a remote part of the terminal. As I approached them, I realized that they were fellow Americans. When I asked them if they were on the Grand Circle trip to Oporto they answered affirmatively. Somehow, we managed to find our gate after a lot of mutual grousing about how confusing things were.

Early on during the 4 or 5 days that we were in Oporto, Ari and his wife Hede suggested that I join the other members of the Lisbon-confused group for cocktails before dinner. I reluctantly agreed (according to Ari). Thus, a daily ritual was established. The mix of the group was kind of interesting. Ari and Hede were natives of Germany but naturalized U.S. citizens. Ari was an engineer by training in postwar Germany while Hede finished a course in fashion design. They owned and managed a cutlery business in Fremont Ohio. Dave and his wife, Bobbie, were a couple from New Bern N.C. He was a retired engineer and she was a housewife. Both were avid golfers. Sally was also a housewife who spent summers with her husband on a lake near Harrison Maine. And, of course, there I was, the black guy from Gainesville Florida. Early on in our pre-dinner cocktail hour, Ari assumed his self-appointed role as "enfant terrible". He tried several avenues of insults and put-downs directed at me. Well, what he did not know was that after a couple of drinks, I could usually hold my own. He finally made a statement to the effect that I had to be o.k. because I could dish as well as he could. I received the Ari Eickert seal of approval that day.

Based upon information revealed during our impromptu self-catered pre-dinner cocktail hours, it turned out that Ari came as close to being a true renaissance man as anyone that I have come across.   Artist(water colors), jazz musician, skier, tennis player, writer, global traveler, history buff; sailboat enthusiast; polylinguist (German, Spanish, English) and entrepreneur.   Hede either fully participated in his endeavors; fully supported them; or initiated other activities in which all or part of the family participated.

A year after our Spain and Portugal trip, all 6 of us met for a long weekend in Maine at Sally and Bill's lake house. Bill, Sally's husband, was either retired navy or coast guard who didn't like to travel. During this trip, besides eating fresh lobster, I also found out that the local McDonalds routinely served lobster rolls that were affordably priced. We were also taken to L.L. Bean's retail store among other places. A year or so later, we all met for a long weekend in Fremont Ohio visiting with the Eickerts. While in Ohio, we traveled to Amish-majority Holmes County, the Rutherford B. Hayes Presidential Center, lunched at the Port Clinton Yacht Club, sailed on Lake Eire, and traveled by bass boat from their home pier to the junction of the Sandusky River and Lake Erie among other activities. Dave became seriously ill during the next summer and passed away. So our group was reduced by one. Both the Joneses and the Eickerts were models for long term commitments in marriages (a topic about which I know absolutely nothing).

The next year, despite my protestations, the remaining group of 4 insisted on coming to Gainesville to spend a weekend with me. I tried my darnedest to impress them as to the lousiness of the idea, how it would turn out poorly at best, how I would be the worst host that they ever encountered.   All of my counter-arguments were to no avail. For their visit, I scheduled a two-hour cruise on the Withlacoochee River with lunch at a riverside restaurant that included fried alligator (never again). Days prior to the group's arrival in Gainesville, I had arranged for a chef whom I knew to enter my house while we were gone in order to prepare a Spanish/Portuguese themed dinner replete with matched Iberian wines for each course. Even my coffee table was covered with a red and gold toro-scene table cloth. Chilled Iberian wine with olives and almonds for appetizers rounded out the starters. A black cast iron candelabra with lit-candles sat at the center of the coffee table. The chef and her assistant pulled out all of the stops for a very memorable dinner. Before dinner I gave the group a brief tour of Gainesville including the neighborhood where I was born and grew up.

I recently dubbed these friendships as "The Improbable Friendships". Among our differences are race, political preferences, and money. I am the only black in the group. I am the only liberal in the group (Hede and Ari describe themselves as libertarian/conservatives). As to money, I can only infer substantial differences with me being on the lowest end of the scale. I don't live on a golf course with membership in the club as Bobbie and Dave did before he passed away. I don't have a lakeside villa as a second home as does Sallie and husband, Bill. I have neither a sail boat nor a bass boat as do the Eickerts. Nor do I live in a sprawling 3 or 4 thousand square foot, understated but exquisitely furnished house on 3 or 4 acres of land situated on a bluff overlooking the Sandusky River. I also don't belong to the tennis and yacht club as do the Eickerts. Despite those differences, we enjoy each others company as long as political discussions are avoided. There are so many other things that we talk about, including travel experiences. That's what happens with friends.

Tales of a Black Sojourner

In conclusion, I am overjoyed that I decided to write this story. My life has been truly enriched by the persons with whom I have established friendships, especially those fostered through the Coffee Breakers. These were people who not only tolerated my idiosyncrasies, they never pulled in the welcome mat, even through my two stormy marriages and divorces. They were tolerant of my rants and never hung up on me. These friendships have withstood the challenges of time. That we continue to care enough about each other to pick up a phone or send an email or send a card after all of this time is nothing less than remarkable. The entirety of the experiences with the people that I have highlighted in this story helped to change me from the angry, sullen, lone and lonely isolated creature that I was into a person who cares about others and demonstrates that care and concern in ways that are acceptable and fairly easy to discern. I am deeply indebted to each of them. Also, as must be obvious, I am really proud of the accomplishments of the individuals that I have described, especially those who are black as am I. Some of us benefited from affirmative action, however, none ever demonstrated any sense of entitlement. We all were or are hardworking people with some of us even simultaneously holding down both full-time plus part-time jobs at various times in our lives. So, who among the blacks mentioned in this story fit the stereotype that is thrown around by certain public figures these days? Definitely none of my friends.

Tales of a Black Sojourner

SEVEN YEARS in
ALCOHOLICS ANONYMOUS

Several years ago, a movie came out starring Brad Pitt. The title of the movie was Seven Years in Tibet. Even though Brad is a bit taller than my now 5'7" frame (I literally lost an inch of height over the years) and has blonde hair (I had hair when younger, even an afro.), by stretching it a bit I had one thing in common with the title of his movie. While the Brad Pitt character spent 7 years in Tibet, I spent 7 years going to AA meetings while remaining booze-free. This was a self-imposed penance brought about after a 2-day binge of drinking led to an act of violence against my second wife. Leading up to the assault upon her, I felt a burgeoning sense of rage because I was broke and financially unable to get back to my hometown, Gainesville Florida, for Christmas. This is the same Gainesville that I absolutely hated except at Christmas time. My emotional need versus hatred for the place was one of the more profound contradictions in my life. During my pre-teen, teen, and college years, I turned my back and thoughts on Gainesville. I constantly reminded myself over those years that I truly hated the town; the narrowness implicit within the gossip among so many; the judgments imposed by members of the black Christian community; and the hypocrisy so often on display did nothing to improve my opinion of Gainesville at the time.

I remember very little of the violence itself. What I do remember are the State Troopers (New York) being in the Croton-on-Hudson house because the wife had pulled the in-house alarm connected to the nearest State Trooper's barracks. As my head was clearing up, I promised the Troopers that I would be leaving the house on the earliest train that I could catch out of Croton-on-Hudson headed for Manhattan. They asked her whether she wanted to press charges and she said no, thank God. I could have spent time in jail. I could have lost everything if she had said yes-my job, my Board of Pharmacy appointment, and maybe my friends and family. I can almost still feel the guilt and shame and self-pity and disappointment that was going on in my heart and mind that early morning. As promised, I did leave the house and Croton-on-Hudson on the earliest train.

After arriving in the city, I walked from Grand Central Station to the Gramercy Park Hotel where I rented a room. Now, I could stew in my own self-pity and my remorse and my guilt, and my shame unimpeded by other human beings. Fortunately, the Gramercy Park Hotel was close enough to my place of employment, Beth Israel Medical Center that I could walk to and from work every day.

Somehow, I found out about a nearby AA group that met weekly at a location near both the hotel and the hospital. The group was called The Mustard Seed. My anxieties and fears were such that I thought that one drink would send me off the deep end again and who knew what I would have been capable of doing then. At any rate, I got a sponsor, Bob, and agreed with the first of the twelve steps that formed the basis of Alcoholics Anonymous' program for recovery.

FIRST STEP

"We admitted (that) we were powerless over alcohol - that our lives had become unmanageable."

Seven Years of Alcoholics Anonymous

My life, especially my non-work life, had indeed become unmanageable and when I drank after work, one drink was almost never enough. Rational people call this binge drinking. It seemed that the alcohol assumed control of the levers guiding my non-work behavior. In other words, I was a functioning alcohol abuser. Without the structure imposed by the workplace, I was generally at loose ends and many times did not want to stop drinking after one drink. Sometimes, after a couple of leisure time drinks, I became witty and funny and the life of the party. If more drinks followed, I could flip between nasty and sarcastic. More drinks could progress (regress?) toward rage and tearful bouts of self-pity. The morning after a binge could be a real bitch with symptoms of nausea, vomiting, headache, and lots of remorse. My suffering was such that I made (and later broke) many a promise to never drink again.

After I attacked my wife, not only did I keep up with weekly AA meetings, I also continued seeing a psychotherapist. The one constant among the successive psychotherapists that I saw was that they kept leaving New York for other places. Seth left Brooklyn because Los Angeles beckoned. Saul left for Miami because he seemed to have significant problems of his own. When I showed up at his Saturday-only St. Regis Hotel suite office in Manhattan, Saul seemed to be under the influence of some agent and was almost incoherent. Another gentleman who came to the door with Saul told me that Saul was in no shape to conduct my session and this Yale Medical School professor (Saul) was ending his New York City practice effective that day. Undaunted by Saul's departure, I later started counseling sessions with Charlotte, a licensed social worker.

While in self-imposed exile, the wife would call me at work and quietly ask when was I coming back home? For nearly 2 weeks, I did not have an answer for her. An incredibly annoying practice of hers was to clam up on the other end of the phone and offer no positive suggestions as to how we might move forward as a healing couple. Attempts at couple sessions with the psychiatrist collapsed during the first meeting because she said that he took my side in respective issues. She was so offended by her perception that she walked out of the session shortly after it had begun. This response came from a woman who had a master's degree in psychiatric nursing.

Even though I returned to the house in Croton-on-Hudson, there was an awful lot of unresolved stuff that only got worse. Here are just a few examples that, in my mind, helped to render the coup-de-grace to our marriage.

I dug up and replanted a rhododendron plant a few feet away from the root system of a large tree in the front yard of the house because the tangle of roots was impeding growth of the plant. Within a couple of hours I looked out of the window and saw her digging up the plant to return it to its original stymied-growth position. Her face was contorted with rage.

About three months after moving into the Croton house, I realized that the wife's promised contribution to household expenses had not been forthcoming. When I reminded her of her promise, she responded with a curt, "Well I guess you have a problem." And I did indeed. A few days later, I presented her with a list of on-going bills that I was no longer going to pay including her most favorite, the telephone. She countered with, "You can't do that". "Watch me!" I said.

The period of her recovery from elective foot surgery coincided with federal income tax reporting time. I had been waiting for the refund check in order to pay taxes on the property. When May rolled around and there was no sign of the refund check, I told her about the situation and my plan to ask IRS to trace whether the refund check had been mislaid. She laughed. On asking her why this issue would engender laughter, she said that a few weeks previously, she had forged my name to the refund check and spent the proceeds to fly to Nashville and Birmingham in order to visit friends and family. She was unemployed during that time. Oh, Boy!

One day, I opened the garage door and saw a brand new Ford sitting beside my car. I made no comment to her. Days later, a bill came from the Ford dealership. The bill was addressed to me. When I contacted the dealership, I let them know that they had made a grave error. I explained that a divorce was in progress and that the car purchase was done without my knowledge. She had used my name and financial data to try and get over, behavior that was typical for her.

While all of the drama, deception, dishonesty, and hatred were frequently on the verge of exploding, I kept my cool, more or less, and continued to go to AA meetings. Frequently, while listening to the stories of various speakers and commentators, I would think that my life had not gotten as bad as theirs. I was momentarily flattered when one of my fellow-AA members would say, "Gene, you are not an alcoholic." While that kind of statement was good for my ego for a little while, it did little to reassure me that I could return to drinking. Fear and anxiety and the absence of confidence in myself were my constant companions especially during non-working hours. All of this domestic drama was clearly indicative of yet another failure in my life.

STEP 2

"Came to believe that a Power greater than ourselves could restore us to sanity."

While I felt rather than knew about the presence of a higher power in my life and the universe, it took me a while to firmly set that "reality" into my skull. Prior to this kind of struggle, I would tell those who would listen that I was an agnostic. Was it Bernard Shaw who supposedly said something to the effect that an agnostic is one who does not have guts enough to declare that there is no God?

One of the regulars that formed the core of Mustard Seed AA attendees was a man named Johnny. I knew nothing of Johnny's origins or his struggles, however, one of my clearest memories of him was his resolve regarding the rather complex issue of the role of a higher power, or Supreme Being, or Creator, or God in guiding him in his everyday life while remaining booze-free. Johnny would say, "I don't understand it." Then he would add, "But I don't got to understand it." No further discourse required. Thanks to AA, Johnny, and others, I became and still am a believer decades later. I continued going to AA meetings while undergoing psychotherapy up until the time that I left New York permanently for the wonderful winter weather of Chicago. I resumed treatment with a Chicago psychotherapist not too long after I settled into my own digs.

Were all of these shrinks helpful to me? Did they help me to survive in A.A.? What part did AA play in maintaining my sobriety? I still haven't figured out the answers to these questions and decades have elapsed since. No matter, I am glad that I stayed the course. I have not been involved in physical violence since that ugly night in 1976'ish Croton. My success with verbal exchanges has been far less exemplary. I have had a tough time peacefully dealing with people who were intent on pushing my buttons. Partners in vitriolic exchanges after my second divorce have included my father and a significant other who would go out of her way to find something critical to say to me. My usual response to such stinging criticisms were almost never one of turning the other cheek. I usually came out swinging.

After 7 years of abstinence I decided to have a couple of gin and tonics while staying at a Great Western Lodge in Vail Colorado where I was spending a ski week. No demons emerged afterwards.

Somewhere along the way while still attending AA meetings, I stopped trying to impose any of the additional 10 steps that form a basis for the remainder of Alcoholics Anonymous' 12 step program. For me, there was a commonality to both psychotherapy sessions and AA meetings. Both allowed me to talk out my issues in the presence of others who were not harshly judgmental. Rather, they were quite supportive while I struggled to sort through and discard some of the emotional baggage that I had allowed myself to accumulate over decades. Now, on most days, I am in a far better place than I was years ago. Alcohol is no longer the catalyst that it was previously in my dealings with others. I'm also far less inclined to preach to others how they should live their lives while I am struggling mightily to improve my own.

RED, GREEN, AND BLACK (?)

I answered the telephone at home one very ordinary day and received an invitation which led to a very extraordinary experience. My friend, Martha Brown, was calling to tell me that her friend and fellow-teacher, Ramona, wanted to invite me to a party that she was giving in her upper Westside Manhattan apartment a couple of Saturdays later. She further informed me that Ramona had a bit of a crush on me after having met me only once before at another party. Her feelings were not reciprocated for some reason. Maybe, the lack of reciprocity might have had to do with the observation that Ramona and my soon-to-be ex-wife were of similar stature, short and stocky.

I arrived at Ramona's apartment on the night of the party and quickly realized that I knew only a couple of people, Ramona, who was busy playing hostess, and Martha, who was otherwise engaged. So, I did what I usually do under such circumstances. I assumed the posture of the Grand Observer. Little did I know that the Grand Observer was being observed. After a while, a young lady approached me and struck up a conversation. She said that her name was Carol and that she was a graduate student at Columbia University pursuing a master's degree in social work. I can't remember how long we talked that night or whether we bothered to dance. Carol and I chatted during the entire party and by the end of the evening I was smitten. Smitten with a capital SMITTEN! What I do remember with some clarity is the feeling that I had over the next couple of days. ENTHRALLED is an apt descriptor. 'GA-GA!' is a phrase that also fit my emotional state. When I thought of her, it seemed that my very soul was on fire.

On the following Monday when I arrived at work, people laughed at the wide grin on my face and wanted to know what was going on with me. I told them about the woman whom I had met at a party over the weekend, a very attractive woman with red hair, green eyes and fair skin. The fact that she was obviously very intelligent made her even more attractive. I assumed that she was "black" since she was attending a party with lots of other black people including myself. Looking back several decades later, it occurs to me that I never asked her whether she was black. Given her skin color, she could have been Scotch or Irish or Italian or an admixture. To me, she was exotica personified and she had picked me out from all of the other dudes present at the party. What flattery!

I can't remember how many times that I called Carol after the party. I can't even remember her last name. We went out a couple of times while I was in my SUPER-SMITTEN phase. One evening, we agreed that she would come over to my apartment in Brooklyn Heights from her home on the upper Westside of Manhattan. When the date for Carol's visit finally came I welcomed her arrival and looked forward to a special evening. Our visit had barely begun when it was interrupted by the buzzing of the intercom. I was more than surprised when I answered and the doorman told me that Mrs. Mills was on her way up. I was also more than annoyed at the doorman's assumptions as I waited for the soon-to-be-ex Mrs. Mills to arrive at the door to inform her that she was not welcome. The doorbell rang. When I opened the door, there stood Samantha (not her real name) in the doorway. My immediate response was uncamouflaged unpleasantness and hostility. Samantha demanded to know who my guest was and what business did she have in my apartment. My near-ex acted as if she had some rights within my bachelor pad as she had in the St. James Place apartment in which we both had lived before I left her.

I don't remember what threat I used to get rid of Samantha. But she did finally leave before there was any blood shed or bruises inflicted. To my great disappointment and after profuse apologies on my part, Carol left soon afterwards. The next day, I called Carol. She informed me that she had no intention of getting serious (or words to that effect). Carol added that the only reason that she came over and started talking to me during the party was that she thought that I was the most interesting looking man in the room. (Maybe it was my afro, beard, mustache, and hazel eyes that caught her attention) She demanded that I never call her again. For some reason, I promised her that I would comply with her demand and never bothered her again.

For the first time in my adult life that I can recall, I felt that I had truly been in love. I believed that what I experienced with Carol was love, no matter how briefly it lasted. Perhaps, it was this acknowledged love that helped me to minimize the time that I spent in grieving over losing her. Perhaps, recognizing and accepting the love that I had experienced made it possible for me to be able to move on with the rest of my life.

MAGICAL POWERS OF PLUCKED NUTRIA?

St. Croix V.I.

Ruth Ann (or Ruthie, the names that I have substituted for my second wife's real name), was a scrapper in a silent withholding kind of way. Silence was her weapon of choice. I on the other hand could be regularly relied upon to act out with the crazies - yelling, door slamming, feeling sorry because I had allowed my own insecurities to dictate another major bad change in my life, drinking, and sulking. I wanted /needed companionship and affection. Regular sex would certainly go a long way towards addressing what writer Alexander King called, "crotch security", mine.

I was not in love with Ruthie but somehow tried to convince myself that a black male and a black female of above average intelligence, both of whom being professionals could find a way to navigate the emotional stuff. After all, she had finished a master's degree in psychiatric nursing while we were still seeing each other. At the same time, I was finishing up a master's degree in pharmacy at Long Island University's Brooklyn College of Pharmacy. I mean, what is not to like about this picture? After all, in India, it was said that about 95% of marriages are arranged marriages.

Not included in my rationalizations were the probable "emotional ages" for each of us. For example, when the female judge threw my divorce case out of court the first time while I was trying to rid myself of first wife, Samantha (not her real name either), I was outraged at the judge. I was also pissed off at my attorney because he had never hinted that I was required to lie, to perjure myself under oath in court that my first wife had a pattern of physically abusing me. (Say, what?) When I later tried to convey my sense of betrayal and disappointment to Ruth Ann, her reaction was to verbally attack me for not having been more successful in the courtroom. She carried on quite a bit about me having broken my promise to divorce wife number one and marry her. The more she carried on the more pissed I became. No where in her histrionics was there any concern about the impact of the courtroom incidents on my emotional state. The traditional tender loving care associated with nursing and nurses was nowhere to be found. She simply wanted to become the new Mrs. Mills and she was not going to put up with any of my sniveling bullshit that would circumvent her from achieving her goal. It was all about status with her. She wanted this afro-headed (This occurred in early 1970's), beard-wearing, mustachioed, hazel-eyed, not-bad-looking, 5'8" black pharmacy director at a major New York City medical center to carry her into black married middle-class status. My emotions be damned! Nevertheless, my insecurities were such that I still wanted to get married again hoping that the hundreds of dollars that I was spending on psychotherapy would somehow bring me to wholeness and life would be wonderful forever after.

For a long time before I ever met Ruth Ann, I knew that my growing up years of being emotionally disconnected from both parents (or so I thought) and my father's seeming indifference through most of my life before overt hostility and competition (his, mainly) set in, I knew that the pain, and hurt, and anger that I continued to feel did not bode well for me when it came to a healthy relationship with any significant other. I lied to myself often when drinking and feeling needy that good health was just around the corner if only my significant other would just make a few needed changes. HAH! I decided to marry Ruth Ann anyway after the divorce of wife number one was complete. Not only did we set a date but I arranged for a small reception at New City's La Cote Basque Restaurant. (They had a prix fixe lunch that I could afford.) I got stuck for all of the costs. Ruth Ann's family could not or would not contribute a single dime to cover the costs despite the fact that several of them were in attendance, including Ruth Ann's 90 plus year-old mother. No matter, the wedding and reception lunch took place.

The next day, it was on to Mexico and THE honeymoon. It became pretty obvious even during our honeymoon in Merida, the Yucatan, and Cozumel Mexico that I had made my second big matrimonial mistake. If I had to leave her for a short period (with explanation of purpose) by the time that I returned, she would be surrounded by small crowds of strangers. It was as if she was silently screaming, "Please save me from being alone with this man that I just married." Actually, had I been more honest with myself and her, the marriage would never have taken place. I was looking for a mate that would soothe my pained psyche and believe in me, allowing my demons to finally be placed at rest. See, the emphasis was all about what she could and should do for me, theoretically. Making matters worse, was the nightmare that I had in the middle of the night while we were both in bed in our hotel room in Merida. I dreamed that a man dressed in feathers was coming at me with a raised stone knife to cut my heart out just as the Mayans had done to their sacrificial victims. My loud scream woke me up and scared hell out of my new bride. Even afterwards, I failed to pick up on the possible symbolism of the threatening man who was determined to cause me unspeakable harm before I died very soon thereafter. Was this symbolism really going to represent my relationship with Ruthie?

We returned to New York and started to do some of the things newlyweds have to do. Ruth Ann had her heart set on living in Peter Cooper Village, the middle-class multi-building rental apartments then owned by Metropolitan Life Insurance Company. Even the one-bedroom apartments were quite spacious and could legally accommodate self-purchased window-mounted air-conditioning units. Because the property was located on Manhattan's Lower Eastside it was within walking distance of my job. While there was a lengthy waiting list when I applied, somehow my application was prioritized and we were able to move in and set up house by the time that we returned from Mexico.

For several days after our return, there was more evidence to convince me that I had made another bad life choice. When I returned home after work, the apartment was almost always darkened with Ruth Ann being in bed and silent. These were daylight hours. And no, there was no implied invitation for me to join her in bed. These conditions were expressions of her depression over the reality of being married for the first time. "I want to be married but I don't want this nutty black guy that I would rather not even look at." Such appeared to be the message that she was silently sending me. Home conditions did nothing positive for my "crotch security" either.

Now, what were some of the things that I was looking for, theoretically, in a marriage? Oh, yeah! Companionship and affection! What I actually got during the weeks ahead was a pretty cold and frightened individual who had far more problems with intimacy than I did. And I thought that I was the one with fairly severe emotional baggage. Added to this mix of environmental toxicity were issues of territoriality, control, honesty, and personal responsibility. Despite being employed, Ruth Ann wanted me to assume responsibility for payment of household bills while she would be free to do as she pleased with her income. Her character was such that even something as simple as the return of overdue public library books was an opportunity to get over on the system. If she could cheat and get away with it, the more the better.

The reality of a couple living in a one-bedroom apartment is that there is no place available to escape from each other, a much-needed respite especially when two strong personalities were involved. After trying to cope with this bit of awareness for several months, it became clear that one of us was going to commit homicide if we didn't get more space and soon. We briefly discussed house ownership vs. condo/co-op ownership. Ruth Ann's preference, naturally, was for the more likely expensive option - a house. After buying a car(again, using only my credit data) we began looking for a house in New Jersey and Westchester County, Ruth Ann's preferred locations. While looking at a super neat Cape Cod house in Hastings-on-Hudson that was above our budget, Ruth Ann commented that she was going to "get this house". Realizing the game that she was already into, I bade her, good luck, and left her standing at the top of the stairs.

Finally, we located a house in the village of Croton-on-Hudson in Westchester County. It was private, attractive, and affordable, in part, because the second floor had not been finished. While preparing the mortgage application, Ruth Ann dropped a bombshell on me. She said that I should only use my financial data because she had declared bankruptcy before I met her. At no point previously while we were repeatedly going over combined income and expense information had she ever mentioned this little fact. I reacted in my usual nearly-out-of-control fashion because she had remained secretive about this little important bit of information.

The stresses of spending weekends searching for an affordable house, Ruth Ann's bombshell, and my being worried that my income alone was going to be insufficient were taking a toll on me. By the time that the approval came through and ownership was transferred in the closing process, I felt that my psyche was as taut as any closed jack-in-the-box toy. If I couldn't get away for a while, I thought that that potential nervous breakdown was finally going to happen and it wasn't going to be pretty. So, despite my worries about money, and despite our very rocky relationship and total inability to calmly discuss and resolve issues, I booked 2 airline seats to St. Croix Virgin Islands and a week's stay for 2 at a condo/hotel just outside of Christiansted.

Ruth Ann had a morbid fear of flying. Her pre-flight ritual consisted of taking 20mg (YES, 20mg) of Valium washed down with 2 martinis. She insisted on doing both in the waiting lounge bar prior to our flight to St. Croix. Instead of the combination knocking her on her ass and/or her becoming comatose and requiring emergency medical intervention, she became the near personification of "La Diva". An ankle-length plucked nutria fur cape and a burgeoning afro completed the image. To finish it off, there was something a little bit haughty about Ruth Ann anyway, even while in a booze-less state. Maybe that was part of the persona of a young black woman who had been allowed to attend undergraduate nursing school at Meharry Medical College. Another probable factor was that Ruth Ann was the youngest of the ten offspring of a Baptist preacher.

After we were airborne, Ruth Ann seemed to not only occupy the aisle seat next to my middle seat, her personality seemed to expand into the spaces surrounding her seat. While watching this transformation, I was torn between trying to pretend that I did not know this woman sitting next to me and being utterly fascinated by this profound personality change.

Seated across the aisle from Ruth Ann was a man who introduced himself as Bob Wolff. He said that he worked in Christiansted and had his office in the downtown area. Somewhere early on in their cross-aisle conversation, Bob seemed to have convinced himself that Ruth Ann was really the singer, Dionne Warwick and that she was trying this incognito bit in economy class with her manager-husband, me. Apparently, Bob's judgment was clouded and he just couldn't seem to get his head beyond the ankle-length plucked nutria cape. Had the nutria cape acquired some magical powers that caused people to see what they wanted to see? Even people seated in the row of seats just ahead of us began giving us slight knowing smiles as if they too, were caught up in the mischief. No protestations on my part about my really being a New York City pharmacist and Ruth Ann being a nurse were going to change Bob's mind.

The conversation between Bob and Ruth Ann lasted the duration of the entire flight. Included in the conversation was the name of the condo/hotel at which we had a reservation. After arriving at the hotel and putting bags away, we decided that we could use a drink and headed to the patio bar. By this time, effects of the Valium/martini concoction had worn off and Ruth Ann was back to her normal self. The man who delivered our drinks was not the same one who took our order. It turned out that our "server" was none other than the manager of the complex. While placing the drinks down at our table, he turned his head slightly towards Ruth Ann and said in a sotto voce manner, "Your secret is safe with me." With that, he turned and walked away. Things got a bit more interesting after we returned to the room. The phone rang. It was Bob Wolff. He wanted to know whether we would be interested in joining him the next day at his downtown second floor office to watch the Three Kings Day parade. He would pick us up and bring us back. Both of us readily agreed. The next day Bob came by and delivered on his promise. He also confirmed that he had called the condo/hotel manager and informed him of the "special guests" at his establishment.

Not only did we watch the parade from the second floor balcony, we were also treated to an unremembered number of tasty successive drinks (probably rum-based) prepared in what appeared to be 12oz glasses. At one point while the action below was in full swing, Bob pointed to a guy in fake pirate's regalia. He said that the fake pirate was one of his friends whose name was Carl Roebuck, a native islander married to an Australian nurse, Sandy, both of whom lived in the same complex where we were staying.

Later, Bob contacted us saying that we were invited to a party that Carl and Sandy were having the next night at their condo. We gladly accepted the new invitation as well. Was this just the work of a deluded man or were the powers of the nutria cape at work? No matter. The hospitality and generosity of the islanders were on full display while Ruth Ann and I were among the willing beneficiaries.

The next night's party guests represented quite a mix of islanders. Besides the hosts, Carl and Sandy, there was Bob, who had almost assumed the role of our social secretary. Other guests included a retired CBS studio orchestra musician; an attorney (can't remember his name), and Charles (Nick) Nixon. Surprisingly, Nick, who was originally from Smithfield, NC, had been a freshman with me at Xavier University, my alma mater. During our second year of pharmacy school, word got around that Charles Nixon had not been allowed to return to Xavier because of poor academics. But here was Nick, 22 years later, a successful pharmacist and businessman. He owned 2 pharmacies. In partnership with his wife, a nurse, they co-owned a hospital on the island based on information that one of the other guests had told us. So much for the real-life effects of one institution's assessment of poor academics.

While the party was going full blast, someone mentioned that the group should spend the next day on Buck Island located about 200 yards or so beyond the main island of St. Croix. The official name for this entity is Buck Island Reef National Monument.

At the appointed meeting time the next day, 3 boats were loaded in the hotel/condo marina (I think) with all kinds of food and booze and bodies. At least one of the pilots knew how to find the opening in the reef which would allow access to Buck Island and its beach. The company was great. The food and booze were great and so was the snorkeling. Unfortunately, Ruth Ann and I continued to behave as free-loading guests. We contributed absolutely nothing to anyone to cover at least a part of the costs of our participation. In the meantime, I did not know to what degree that Bob was still spellbound by the ankle-length plucked nutria cape.

As expected, temperature on the island was quite warm (this all took place in the first week of January) so there was no reason for Ruth Ann to continue to wear the cape. Given all of the terrific surprises that Bob was able to arrange for us, I don't remember there being any further discussions about our real identities - the real identities of both Ruth Ann and me. It was as if events were evolving and unfolding in ways that seemed to be guided by some unknown hand or force. Fortunately, there was serendipity in that good things repeatedly happened to us without our asking.

The lawyer whom we met for the first time at Sandy's and Carl's party decided that he would volunteer to be our personal guide and chauffeur. So the day after the party, he came by our room, picked us up and provided a tour and commentary of sites around the entire island. It was through this gentleman that we got to see Fredericksted, the next largest town on the island. Again, I cannot recall the reason that he went to such extraordinary measures of generosity. Try as I might, I cannot remember the attorney's name.

There was still more in store for us. We met a gentleman who owned a furniture store or stores in some part of Michigan. I cannot remember where or how we met but he insisted that we join him and his entourage for dinner at a local restaurant. I just have very small snatches of memory from that evening.

Maybe the most surprising and special thing that happened during our trip to St. Croix is that Ruthie and I kept the peace between us during the entire week. We did not fight or have a disagreement during the entire 7 days. While other details of our visit remain foggy at best, the highlights of that incredible week were marked by the remarkable generosity, hospitality and acceptance of two previously unknown people, Ruth Ann and me, by people whom we had just met.

Maybe the plucked-nutria ankle-length cape had no special powers but it certainly got the attention of the man who was behind a lot of the pleasant and enjoyable experiences that made this one of the most extraordinary trips that I have ever taken. So, Bob Wolff, here's to you wherever you are.

THE VERDICT and IT'S CONSEQUENCES

Over the course of a few short weeks, I had been poked, probed, stabbed, scooped (biopsy) and manipulated. Even my most private of spaces had not been spared these sometimes painful onslaughts. Worst of all, this invasion occurred at the hands of and in the presence of total strangers. Here I was miserably and repeatedly failing to measure up to a commonly held stereotype of black adult males. Oh! The shame of it all. Oh! The indignity of it all!

You've probably heard the clue "biopsy" to figure out that I was not the battered victim of a criminal assault. I faced, instead, a situation that was much worse. In fact, tentative assessments of the various medical tests to which I had been subjected had already started to raise alarming signals.

My follow-up appointment to discuss the results of the tests with a urologist was scheduled for 11 o'clock on Friday morning. During this appointment, all would be revealed. I would finally hear the verdict. Needless to say, I had built up a huge amount of anxiety about what conclusions had been drawn from the test results. Looking back over my daily journal entries, I find several references to my unusually high level of anxiety leading up to the verdict. As an aside, in contrast to normal people, I have had more than my share of behavior fueled by an overactive (but not creative) imagination.

The Verdict and It's Consequences

Because I only allowed 30 minutes to travel from my home in Northwest Gainesville to Shands Medical Plaza on the opposite end of town, I simply hadn't included enough time to find a parking slot in the patient parking facility and walk the nearly block-long distance from parking facility to the third floor of the Medical Plaza building. As I hurried along, I was once more reminded as to how complex Shands Healthcare facilities are, especially if one is a patient requiring access to one of the many clinical locations. Despite this latest self-imposed challenge, I arrived at the urology clinic only a few minutes after 11 o'clock. No one seemed to have noticed my moments of tardiness. Absent was any stern-faced staff member waiting to reprimand me for my level of patient malfeasance.

There were eight or ten people seated in the waiting area when I arrived. A nearly visible large-screen television monitor was affixed to one wall several feet away to my right. Despite the fairly muted volume, I occasionally took a glance at the TV screen in order to find out what miserable events had transpired since I had checked various news websites earlier in the morning.

Fifteen, twenty, thirty, forty-five minutes rolled by without my name being called. After more than an hour, a woman dressed in scrubs emerged from the inner sanctum and announced that the patients waiting to see the urologist would have to wait for another half-hour or so as the practitioner was about an hour or so behind schedule. Needless to say, this unplanned delay did absolutely nothing to allay my level of anxiety. Indeed, I became even more anxious the longer I waited. Running through my head were thoughts like this: I have waited all of this time to get my verdict and the universe has chosen to play games with me. I've done terrible deeds earlier in my life and this delay is karmic payback. And OK. The verdict is going to be really bad. Otherwise I would not have had to wait this long. For some unknown reason, when my mind is given choices, it tends to settle on the worst of possibilities.

Finally, after about an hour and a half, my name was called by a clinic staff member. Then, after waiting another half-hour or so in a small exam room with closed door, the urologist came in with an attractive twenty-something young female whom he introduced as his physician-assistant. My first thought was, "Oh no! I do hope that they are not going to invade my private spaces again." As things developed, my invasion fears were relieved when the only touches were a couple of handshakes.

Immediately afterwards the real boom was lowered by the urologist. "I am sorry that I don't have good news for you.", he said. "The pathologist has confirmed that you have cancerous lesions in your prostate gland. The CT scan confirms that the cancer has spread to adjacent lymph nodes." He added that a bone scan would have to be done in order to determine whether the cancer had spread to my bones. Unfortunately, the bone scan would have to be scheduled for another date. The urologist went on to discuss possible treatment options for this the most aggressive type of prostate cancer according to microscopic cellular characteristics. Options included daily radiation therapy as determined by a radiation oncologist plus hormonal therapy ordered by the medical oncologist. Appointments with these two specialists could not be done immediately and I would again have to play the waiting game. So, the verdict based upon all of these clinical parameters was LOUSY and possibly getting worse by the week.

The Verdict and It's Consequences

The bone scan needed for a complete diagnosis was completed and I waited for the results. The very welcome news was that the bone scan did not show any spread of the cancer beyond the prostate and adjacent pelvic lymph nodes. This was positive news. WHEW!

After the verdict was reached and the treatment plan established, I requested that treatment be delayed until I had completed my 12-day trip to Cuba with the Grand Circle Foundation. The radiation oncologist agreed, however, the medical oncologist felt that I should receive the first dose of leuprolide before my departure. My feelings were mixed about this timing. What if I should start to experience side effects, which can range from mild to completely debilitating, from the leuprolide while I was in Cuba? With a leap of faith, I agreed to administration of the drug before traveling. Fortunately, there were no troublesome events that occurred during the trip.

I wish that I could say the same about the 44 days of pelvic radiation that started after my return from Cuba. The name that I invented for the cluster of symptoms that occurred due to pelvic radiation therapy was The Three B's Syndrome - symptoms involving the bladder, bowels, and bleeding (rectal). Added to the three B's were night sweats which probably were consequences of non-compliance with CPAP use for the treatment of diagnosed chronic obstructive sleep apnea. The night sweats would occur regularly two to four times per night and were so heavy at times that I would have to change the tops of my sleep gear. Radiation-induced bladder inflammation caused urinary frequency, delayed initiation of urine stream, partial emptying of bladder, incontinence, and urinary urgency. Bowel damage showed up as alternating waves of constipation and diarrhea. Bouts of constipation brought about straining, sweats, and rectal bleeding from previously existing hemorrhoids. Because of the inflamed condition of both bowels and bladder, sphincters became very unreliable at times. I often had to operate on the basis of what I called the sixty-second rule of bladder/bowel hygiene. The sixty-second rule held that immediately after the first urge to go to the bathroom, I had about sixty seconds to get to the throne and sit. It didn't matter where I was sitting, standing, or what I was doing when the countdown started. If my response time was lousy, sphincters would loosen of their own volition and I would have to spend time cleaning up and changing clothes. One day, I had to change clothes three times.

Being someone who embarrasses fairly easily, such episodes were bad enough when they happened while I was alone at home. However, on one occasion, this bowel urgency occurred at the beginning of a radiation therapy session just as I had been positioned on the table but before the balloon catheter was rectally inserted and inflated. With profuse apologies to the therapists, I immediately tried to express the urgency of my situation while begging to be released at once from the table, asking at the same time for the location of the nearest restroom. The anti-diarrheal, Lomotil, had failed me miserably that day. I made it to the restroom with only about a second to spare. TALK ABOUT EMBARRASSMENT IN THE PRESENCE OF OTHERS! Being aware of the tight scheduling that characterized the radiation therapy unit, I became more and more anxious the longer I stayed in the bathroom. Yet, I could not afford to return to the treatment area until I was sure that the bout of diarrhea was well over. Does the rock and a hard place analogy have any relevance in situations like this one?

While none of the symptoms caused by radiation and/or leuprolide therapy were life-threatening, they were certainly at the top of the list of the most annoying, embarrassing, and mentally debilitating events that I've ever experienced, especially when combined with sleep deprivation. One other highly visible effect of the leuprolide is that my midsection is beginning to look like the comic strip character, Wimpy. It seems that I can almost hear the struggle going on between the diminishing number of muscle cells as they lose out to the ever increasing number of fat cells. As a result, I have now gained about 2 more inches of abdominal girth. The air in my master bedroom and bath have bee downright blue from my frequent cussin'. Despite the profane moments, I also frequently prayed to The Creator for healing. For some reason, I still do not find these contradictory emotional states at all unsettling. If anything, these opposites prove that I am a mere mortal whose flaws are all too often on display.

As of this writing, it's been two hundred days since the end of daily radiation therapy. Leuprolide therapy is projected to last over the next two and one-half years with monitoring. Fortunately, PSA and testosterone levels have met treatment expectations. Somehow, at age 79 and romantically unattached, long-term, it doesn't bother me too much that I will be a functional eunuch for the duration of the leuprolide therapy. Choosing contained advanced prostate cancer over a liberated functioning libido is a real no-brainer for me.

CHICAGO - SAUDI ARABIA:

FROM THE FRYING PAN INTO THE FIRE

I was hired as Associate Director of Pharmacy two years before Paul arrived and began his stint as the Director of Pharmacy at Rush Medical Center in Chicago. After Paul's arrival, I continued to do my job as Associate Director of Pharmacy to the best of my abilities despite his efforts to undercut my role and authority. It was not long after his arrival that I began to loathe the backbiting and general work environment. The toxic environment and some of the things that happened to me personally drove me to a point at which I was determined to find employment elsewhere.

In general, the environment was not a good fit for me. Suffice it to say, the Rush model of people in high places tended towards the academic, research-oriented bullshit (mainly). If you could talk the talk of academia you automatically had a leg up. Indeed, one of the favored, acceptable phrases of the Administrative Vice President to whom the Director of Pharmacy reported was "masters-prepared" which was used instead of a question or a statement regarding holding a masters degree. Besides healthcare delivery credentials, many on staff held academic appointments to Rush University which was a part of the medical center. I let it be known that I was not an academic. Rather, I was a pragmatic problem solver. It was a snobbish environment into which I had no business trying to fit myself.

Complicating things, people who reported to me on paper were also reporting directly to Paul. He frequently complained about some of us not doing anything while he was away. The great irony was that Paul spent about half of his time traveling and probably pulling down extra bread in the process. Relating a few incidents will help to tell the story of the negative environment, Paul's egomania and his personal hostility toward me.

Several days before Christmas, I found a greeting in my departmental mailbox that said, "Red and green are the colors of Christmas, black is the color death. Die nigger!" Of course, there was no signature on the card. It had been placed in my mailbox by hand which strongly suggested that the perpetrator of this hate mail was someone within the department. Neither the Assistant Director of Security (who was black and held the position for a long time) nor Paul (Italian-American) thought that the card was in any way significant. Indeed, Paul became angry with me for having shown him the card. He concluded that the real problem was that I was too sensitive. This was a charge that he had leveled at me on more than one occasion.

In addition to the personal animosity toward me that Paul displayed, he was more than unhappy with me being in the position that I was in and he showed it. At times, I wondered whether he had a problem with me being the highest ranking black person in the department. He tried to belittle me during a manager's meeting one day by telling the group that I was probably gay. There were probably 10 or 12 other people sitting around the conference room table at the time that he voiced his suspicion. I sat in my seat seething and embarrassed but said nothing at the time. I think that I feared losing my job if I had freely responded to Paul's totally inappropriate statement. There were several other incidents in which it appeared that Paul really had a hard time deciding what to do with me or what to make of me. At one point, he seemed to conclude that I was responsible for cleanliness of the men's room in the department which was located just a few feet away from his office. In the meantime, I was keeping score and trying to use lessons learned the hard way in my previous position. Equation? Too sensitive equates to queerness?

I had come to Rush from a position as Director of Pharmacy at Beth Israel Medical Center in New York, where I had tried vainly to fit myself into the environment and carry out my responsibilities through a staff of over 50 people. Ultimately, my efforts were ineffective. I was fired after 19 years, with at least the last three being adversarial. Perhaps I forgot that I was a black male department head trying to survive in a Jewish-controlled organization. I should have seen the handwriting on the wall when one day, my immediate boss, Danny Zipkin, told me that his boss, Lynn Lorch, was "after my ass". He wanted to know what I had done to Lynn. When Danny was promoted, there was a change in administrative responsibilities and I began reporting to Howard (last name forgotten). It seems that Howard had been given instructions that I was to be treated like dirt. He began a campaign of verbal abuse. I played the race card as a means of getting him off my back but it backfired miserably eventually.

Exacerbating the vitriol directed against me by Howard was an incident in which Lynn Lorch demanded that I commit an illegal act because he had instructed me to do so. When I told him no, in no uncertain terms, he became angry and ordered me to choose between upholding the conditions necessary for maintaining my pharmacist's license or submitting myself unquestioningly to his authority. He only got angrier when I chose the former. Irony of ironies is that Lynn would have been the first person to report me to the New York State Board of Pharmacy for rules violations or had me fired immediately had I followed his order. Things went downhill fairly rapidly after that and I was later fired. Despite precipitating a profound sense of failure, the firing allowed me to begin to unravel my identity and sense of self from the position of Director of Pharmacy. I promised myself afterwards that I would never again overstay my welcome on any job.

My experience in New York was a good teacher and I used the knowledge and insight gained there to deal with the situation at Rush. It had become clear that no welcome mat existed for me and my role within the department. Having smarted up a little bit, I began looking around for a means of escape.

I even considered changing my profession until a career counselor laid out possible outcomes of starting at the bottom again in another profession.

One day, I saw a classified ad in a professional journal for a Director of Pharmacy at the 250-bed King Khaled Eye Specialist Hospital in Riyadh, Saudi Arabia. The listed recruiting office was located in Beverly Hills, California. I sent my resume to the address that was provided. About a week later, I received a telephone call from someone who asked whether I was really interested in the director's position. My answer was a resounding, YES! Days later, I received an airline ticket and a note that stated that a room was reserved for me at the Beverly Hilton. I flew out for the interview and got a favorable verbal response. A couple of weeks later, I received a call verifying that I had been hired. A mail confirmation followed.

Until that point, I had kept all of these transactions secret. It gave me great pleasure to write a very short note of resignation, effective in four weeks. Paul was away from his desk at the time that I left the note. Shortly afterwards, Paul stormed into my cubicle of an office demanding to know what was going on with my note of resignation. What followed was very ugly, even obscene. With the door closed, I unloaded all of the pent up anger, rage, frustration, and unhappiness that I had experienced over a two-year period. To his face, I called him out for being a disrespectful, non-supportive, near-racist, egocentric, intimidating bully among other things. Every charge that I hurled at him was laced with the most vile four, five, and six letter epithets that I had in my mental lexicon. My emotional state was in hyperdrive. I held back NOTHING because I had nothing to lose. What the hell was he going to do, not give me a recommendation for my next job? Hell no! I got the job totally on my own which probably pissed him off even more. I yelled at him. I got in his face. I cursed at him so much that my mouth ran dry. I excused myself to find some badly needed water. When I returned, Paul was still sitting where I had left him. I again shut the door to my office and restarted my tirade against him.

In some ways, there was a power shift and I was dominant and in control during those moments. He was powerless to retaliate against me because I was leaving soon for another job over which he had no influence whatsoever. IT FELT SOOO GOOD!

On my last day of work at Rush, Paul apparently gave orders that none of the hundred plus staff members was allowed to attend the cake and ice cream goodbye party that the secretarial staff had insisted on giving me despite my strenuous objections.

Besides the secretaries, no one else came, not even Paul. What he did not know, apparently, was that I did not give a shit one way or the other. This was it! I was out of there! My wishes, my dreams, my escape were now fully realized, or so I thought at the time.

A few days later, after most of my possessions had been picked up from my apartment and put into storage, I flew from Chicago to New York for a couple of days visiting friends. I then caught a flight to Riyadh on Saudia Airlines, a 15+ hour non-stop flight. I had arranged to have my apartment rented while I was out of the country.

For the first time in my professional life, I set 3 objectives for myself before leaving the U.S. The first objective was to save money (easily achievable because there was little to spend money on in Saudi Arabia). The second objective was to travel to foreign destinations that would be too expensive for me had the travel originated in the U.S. The third objective was to compare work-place conditions/environments in a foreign country to see if they would be as contentious and adversarial and toxic and shitty as my experiences had been in the U.S.

On arriving in Riyadh, after clearing immigration and customs, I was met by a hospital representative to whom I immediately had to surrender my passport which he would later give to my employer as required by Saudi labor law. I can't remember what the personal identity document looked like that had to be used locally in lieu of my passport. At any rate, I was taken from the airport to the walled multiple-building compound where the apartment block that contained my assigned 2 bedroom fully furnished air-conditioned apartment was located.

My arrival in Riyadh coincided with a Saudi weekend. Instead of work schedules carving out Saturdays and Sundays for weekends as is done in the U.S., Saudi Arabian weekends consisted of Fridays and Saturdays. Devout Muslims in the country attended services in mosques on Fridays. Arriving on a weekend allowed me some breathing room before meeting the new (to me) staff and getting started on my new gig. At this time, I was filled with hope, ambition, and confidence that I was in the right place at the right time.

For the life of me, I cannot remember the circumstances that surrounded my first encounter with Ahmed Al-Shammary. Little did I know, initially, that while Al-Shammary's job title was assistant to the superintendent of the hospital he had been allowed to interpret his position as an all-powerful overseer and meddler and even micro-manager. Worst of all, Al-Shammary was a pharmacy school graduate and assumed that he knew best. In his view, I was required to genuflect in his presence before initiating any changes in the department, no matter what the hospital's table of organization delineated. Al-Shammary's interpretation of his role did not appear on any organizational chart that I was ever shown. He was an employee of the Saudi Ministry of Health and I was employed by the American-Saudi company that was contracted to manage the hospital on behalf of the Saudi Government. On a number of occasions, I tried to get a clarification of my role as Director of Pharmacy as opposed to Al-Shammary's role as assistant to the superintendent, Ministry of Health. Apparently, in Al-Shammary's view, I was directly accountable to him AND to hospital administration. Therein lay the conflict.

Chicago – Saudi Arabia

I found out that after I had been employed for just 3 months I could take a week of vacation. Several people whom I had met or spoken to tended to speak very highly of Thailand so I made the big decision to book one week of travel to that country, including the Northern city of Chiang Mai. It seems that fate had arranged for me to see the most beautiful women in the world throughout my travels in the country. Thailand turned out to be the most foreign and exotic location that I had ever visited up until that point. Starting with my Bangkok hotel's lobby, beautiful women were everywhere. Complementing their attractiveness were the traditional silk two-piece garments that so many of them wore. Momma mia!! Standing rule, "Don't touch the silk."

On returning to Riyadh and still reveling in the glow of my first trip to Thailand, I found out that, in my absence, Al-Shammary had given a party for every member of the pharmacy staff (my staff) to show them how much more he appreciated them (versus my indifference, maybe?) and their contributions to the department's objectives. I was flabbergasted at first because I had never experienced anything so blatantly manipulative and disrespectable to me as the department head. So, I went from being flabbergasted to being pissed. I decided that if Al-Shammary really wanted to be the Director of Pharmacy and assistant to the superintendent, I would make things very easy for him by resigning. After all, I had already had enough bullshit from individuals in the work-place and I did not need anymore from any s.o.a.b., native or foreign.

Some time after I had turned in my letter of resignation, one of the Americans warned me about my glaring U.S. tax liability. Because I had been in the country (Saudi Arabia) for less than a year, I was looking at about 3 months of earnings on which I would now have to pay U.S. income taxes. Hmmm! Was I so pissed about what was going on that I was now ready to pay through the nose (wallet)?

108

After a few days, my answer was no. I requested through my boss that my resignation be rescinded. My request for withdrawal of the resignation was accepted.

Since Al-Shammary had been allowed to assume the power that he had amassed and given the absence of boundaries regarding the sort of micro-management that he seemed to enjoy, my challenge was to find a way of working around him without kissing his ass or seeming to. I was not very successful. Clearly he was going to show me who was really in charge and who had the power. To ensure that he was fully aware of what was going on in pharmacy, Al-Shammary would call out pharmacy staff members from their work-place, sit them down, and ask them about my activities. All of this was done without my knowledge. He had set up a secret spy network within my department. Even the American staff members started acting weird. Why should they listen to me when Al-Shammary let them all know that he was indeed, "THE MAN"?

Enough bullshit of the Saudi kind. I secretly marked November 30, 1988 as my last day of employment, provided that I could last that long. At any rate, my earnings would continue to be tax-free because more than one-year would have elapsed with me in the nominal position of Director of Pharmacy as of that date.

One of the few pleasures that I experienced during those turbulent months was sharing lunch with some of the other Americans working in the hospital.

As I began to relate the latest drama in my little soap opera, all of the Americans said that they had never before heard of the kind of struggles that I was having. Some of the Americans had worked in

Saudi Arabia for years off and on in various capacities, yet none of them had ever witnessed anything comparable to the things that I was going through. None of the other Americans that I lunched and socialized with was black.

For example, when I tried to promote another sharp, highly competent, and really slick African-American pharmacist from Supervisor to Assistant Director of Pharmacy, it was blocked. No one would tell me the reason for this refusal or who had blocked the promotion.

In another incident, I worked for a number of weeks on a medical and nursing staff newsletter. Al-Shammary claimed that some one on staff complained about the amount of time that I was spending in the medical library as a part of my effort to use scientifically valid information as a basis for the content of articles that were to be included. I quickly squashed that complaint. Once the newsletter was finished and distributed, I received several compliments from members of the medical staff including some from the Medical Director. These compliments more than made up for some of the nonsense that was going on. They also made Al-Shammary's self-assigned role of hyper critic a bit more difficult.

Having come to realize the extent to which Al-Shammary wanted to keep my face in the mud with him being "The Man", I decided that my game-playing days were over and it was time for me to confirm the date and to act on the decision I had made earlier to leave the country. Hence, my second letter of resignation without having to pay a price for my departure, was effective November 30, 1988. A couple of weeks before that date, however, I quietly requested and received permission from the hospital's Director (for administration), an American, to spend the rest of my time tying up loose ends from an office fairly hidden and quite distant from the pharmacy. My supposed rationale was that I was taking this action so as not to interfere with Al-Shammary's supervision of the pharmacy and its personnel. Only the departmental secretary and the hospital's Director knew where my temporary digs were located.

It was during these last 2 weeks of employment that I heard from one of the Americans that Al-Shammary had told her that the management company had scraped the bottom of the barrel when they chose a black man, me, to head a department of the hospital. For all that I know, I could have been the first black person to head a department at that institution. The other thing that I tended to forget was that slavery was outlawed in Saudi Arabia in 1963, a mere 20 plus years before I arrived on the scene.

During these last 2 weeks, I met with Al-Shammary in his office one time to give him my assessment of where things were in pharmacy at that time. As far as I was concerned, that was the end of any direct involvement with all things related to Al-Shammary. Hence, I was a bit surprised when on the final day of my resignation, I was told that I would not receive either my final paycheck or passport or permission to leave the country until I had "turned over" the department to Al-Shammary. Not being familiar with that term, I asked for clarification. I was told again that I had to turn over the department to Al-Shammary. I received no clarification, only repetition. This impasse lasted from November 30th until December 5th. Al-Shammary had blocked the issuance of my final paycheck and prevented personnel from returning my passport to me as I exited the country for good. It wasn't until I went to see one of the management company's American vice presidents and informed him of my dilemma did this impasse get resolved. A few hours after that conversation, I received a telephone call from the hospital's Director informing me that my final paycheck would be delivered to me personally by 5 o'clock that afternoon and that my passport would be released at the airport upon my exit. The next day, I was on a flight to Bangkok with my passport in my possession. The day after that I was in the office of a Thai travel agent booking flights and hotels to Singapore, Malaysia, Cairns and Sidney Australia, Hong Kong, Los Angeles and Gainesville, Florida. I would be traveling for 5 weeks.

Oh, yes! Here is how I made out with my objectives before leaving for Saudi Arabia.

1. I saved money at a rate that actually scared me, even though I had taken a $7,000 per year cut in pay to take the Saudi job.

2. My travel opportunities did expand with my first visit to Thailand.

3. The one thing that I had not counted on regarding foreign work environments was racism. Given Al-Shammary's statement about being black and therefore unqualified, it fit a pattern that I had been subjected to previously. Lynn Lorch at Beth Israel had told my boss that I was being paid too much money. Was it too much because I was black? Does a white person make too much money? Lynn also said that I had transcended my color and would have no interest in the hiring of another black department head at the hospital. Did such a statement relate to a perception that I was uppity, arrogant and did not know my place?

Bottom line is that my King Khaled Eye Specialist Hospital employment was considerably worse than I had encountered before.

The one thing that Lynn, Paul, and Al-Shammary had in common was that they did not like me as a person and that they wanted to display their disdain by treating me like shit, circumstances to which I do not respond kindly. This despite my efforts to treat others with respect and fairness, working as hard as I could, and being as cooperative as common sense would allow.

These are the words of a survivor. I am 79 years old as this is being written and I am still extremely selective as to how much bullshit that I will take and from whom. I consider myself extremely blessed that I no longer work for anyone for pay. Both Florida pharmacist licenses were retired about two years ago. This decision was arrived at when I realized that even the part-time work that I was doing and enjoying was interfering with my flexibility as to travel planning. My number one priority after eating; car payments; annual real estate taxes; payment of cable TV, telephone, and internet service; credit card payments; etc., is finding the means to make two trips abroad every year. So far, I have been quite successful in that regard, even sandwiching in a couple of cross-country train trips in between. For these, I am truly grateful.

Poor Sam! Poor Stella/J.! Poor Us!

Thinking that Chicago was large enough to provide some kind of job opportunity no matter what might happen in the future at Rush Medical Center, my then employer, I decided that I would look for an affordable condo. At the time, I was paying rent for a 1 bedroom apartment on Gordon Terrace, a street that intersected Lake Shore Drive on Chicago's north side. After 2 years of paying rent, I wanted the tax advantages of home ownership even though living on Gordon Terrace had been a pleasant experience.

In order to accomplish this, I scanned the real estate section of the Chicago Tribune on a daily basis. One day during my search, I saw an ad for a one bedroom apartment located in a high-rise at 3600 Lake Shore Drive. The unit was a bank repo and affordable. I called the real estate agent and we met in the lobby of the building, took the elevator to the 27th floor, and went to the end of the hall. There the agent opened the door to a corner apartment. Inside the apartment, almost everything was a depressingly dark blue. With no exceptions, the chairs, walls, carpet, bedspread, drapes – everything was the blue of unwashed denim jeans. Even though it was daylight outside, no sunlight pierced the apartment's interior. I couldn't wait to get out of there.

I made my sentiments known to Elizabeth, the real estate agent, who had shown me the apartment. Before we parted company, she asked whether I had made a true assessment of the amount of space in the unit. The answer was, no. I had not been able to get beyond all of that dark blue. Having nothing to lose, I agreed to take a closer look, irrespective of my firmly held negative first impression. The second look sealed the deal, in part because the unit had 960 sq. ft. of living space.

When the drapes were opened in the living room and bedroom, the views were spectacular with unobstructed visual access to miles of the northern section of Chicago. This included huge swaths of Lincoln Park and its green spaces on the opposite or lakeside of Lake Shore Drive, a multi-lane highway which approximated the contours of the 17 miles of waterfront of Chicago's part of Lake Michigan. Picture windows, about 5 ft. high, ran the width of both the living room and bedroom. From the window of the master bath, I could see Lake Michigan sunrises. Parts of Wrigley Field could be seen while standing close to the living room windows and looking to the left. In the distance, planes landing and taking off from O'Hare Airport added excitement to the view, especially at night. With the price being right and the views outstanding, my choice was made for me.

After purchasing the apartment and before the painters started to brighten up the space, there was one huge surprise that took place when the carpet was removed. The background floor color was orange. The orange tiles were covered with images of witches replete with pointy hats, black cats and other symbols of either Halloween or the occult. This was a bit unsettling to say the least. I wondered about the history of the folks who had lived in and/or visited the unit. Were there any real connections between the floor imagery and the lives of the people within? I decided to drop such speculation once the apartment was repainted a neutral color and the carpet replaced.

Poor Sam! Poor Stella/J.! Poor Us!

Not too long after moving into my 27ᵗʰ floor digs, I was shopping in the building's small on-site grocery store. A tall black lady approached me and introduced herself as my next door neighbor, Stella. On at least two occasions afterwards, I saw Stella from a distance. On one of these occasions she was getting into her car and was dressed in a white suit and large white hat as if she were on her way to church.

Several months later, I started noticing an odor, an unpleasant and persistent odor. Looking on top of and beneath every object in my apartment, I could find no basis for the odor. It only worsened the longer it lasted. During this time, I happened to meet Mrs. Edelson, the neighbor across the hall. She too was experiencing the same odor problem. My lady friend, Pat, couldn't help noticing the odor during a visit. Initially, she said that she felt that I was literally rotting away but remaining silent about the process. The odor was strongest when I either sat or walked near the wall between Stella's apartment and mine. Not even building management could find the reason for this extremely foul odor.

One evening while returning home from work, there were television trucks, talking heads, production crews and super bright lights all set up in front of my building. When I got off the elevator on my floor and turned towards my apartment, I saw cops all over and around my end of the hall. As I got closer to my door, I breathed a sigh of relief. They were not in front of my door. They were, instead, in and around the apartment next door, Stella's apartment. Having been trained well during my New York years, I looked but kept moving until I was inside my apartment.

I was jogging regularly during those days so I changed into my jogging clothes, took the tunnel underneath Lake Shore Drive, came up into Lincoln Park and commenced my routine. By the time that I got back to my building, the television folks were all still there and my curiosity had reached hyper-drive level. I questioned the concierge as to the presence of all of the cops and media. His response was that someone had "passed away". Before I could ask for a clarification, he looked at me and said, "Mr. Mills, it was your next door neighbor that passed away." Incredulous, I said, "Do you mean Stella?" He smiled and told me that Stella was not my next door neighbor's name. In fact, the neighbor's real name was Jerome. Stella/Jerome was a transvestite. Wow! I was stunned.

Later that night, local television news was filled with reports that described the murder in a "Gold Coast high rise." The next day at work I experienced at least 5 minutes of my 15 minutes of fame when I let it be known to various questioners that the murder victim had been my next door neighbor who had been killed several days before being found. The odor that had bothered me and other residents had been the odor of a dead and decaying human body, Stella/Jerome's body.

Subsequent news reports told stories about what happened leading up to the murder. It seemed that Stella had been in a bar and picked up a guy named Sam Loveless (ain't kidding). They returned to Stella's apartment where, I assume, Sam anticipated that Stella was going to shower her favors upon him that night. Instead, Stella turned the tables, became Jerome and raped poor Sam. Sam probably left Jerome's apartment with more than his manhood and dignity wounded. Later, during the same evening, Sam returned to Jerome's apartment. Tables were turned once more when Sam bludgeoned Jerome to death and left him to rot for weeks until Jerome's body was discovered. Poor Stella/Jerome! Poor Sam! Poor us for neither hearing anything nor figuring out what horrors had taken place right next door.

MI AVENTURA ECUATOREANA

At the outset, I must confess that my Spanish language skills are about at the same level as those of a mentally-challenged Spanish-speaking 3-year-old despite my having taken numerous beginning Spanish lessons over the past several decades. The Spanish title was chosen for this story just to prove that all of that money and all of that time wasn't totally for naught. The translation of the title is my Ecuadorean adventure. I do hope, dear reader, that you are impressed. If not, you will be responsible for a 79 year-old man crying and wailing because of the admission of abject late-age failure. Such an image should melt the hearts of all women, men, and children everywhere.

Now, on to the adventure in progress. Our travel group of 7 had arrived at the airport outside of Quito Ecuador from Cartagena, Colombia during the afternoon of Friday, September 20th (2013). Our tour director, Paul, (pronounced as two syllables locally, i.e. Pa-ool) began to give us the scoop on the city of Quito and the country of Ecuador almost as soon as we had seated ourselves in the very comfortable and roomy minibus for the nearly 1-hour ride into the City. Several times during our tour director's presentations, a certain member of our group of 7 would interrupt the content and flow of the presentation with totally irrelevant and unrelated questions and comments. Let's call this gentleman, Moe, as in the Three Stooges, Larry, Curley, and Moe. While our Colombian tour director, Jairo, had been discrete and low-keyed when he was similarly interrupted during the 12-day Colombian portion of our journey, Paul let Moe know after about 10 minutes that he, Paul, would not tolerate Moe's disruptive and irritating behavior. Paul pointed out to Moe that his behavior was disrespectful to his fellow-travelers. To Paul's credit, his voice came across as one who knew the difference between putting someone down out of anger and retaliation and conveying to someone the message that it was his behavior that was driving other's of us to distraction. Paul's additional advantage was that, even though he was a native of Ecuador, his English was as perfect as that of the other six of us fellow-travelers.

After being told off by Paul, Moe said that he would say nothing more for any reason. He was going to fix Paul and the rest of us by not talking at all. While in Colombia, several of us became pretty fed up with Moe's antics. On the other hand, a number of the women and Wilson were concerned because Moe was traveling by himself and should be made to feel that he was an integral part of the larger group. So, instead of letting Moe fend for himself, they attempted to include him in conversations, meal sharing, etc. Caught up in this dilemma far more than any of the rest of us were the couple, Lois and Wilson Turner of Hanover Virginia. The more they tried to include Moe, the more he seemed to cling to them, even inviting himself to share meals. Barbara, a single traveler from Dallas Texas who had become close with the Turners, seemed to be the object of Moe's earnest intentions. Unfortunately, Moe seemed unable to restrain himself from asking Barbara inappropriate questions and making annoying statements.

Then, there were Moe's eating habits. Watching him eat was a real revolting experience. His attacks on the contents of his plate were unlike anything else that I had ever seen. There was something almost animalistic in the ways in which he used his knife, fork and fingers to attack chicken parts in particular. It was a kind of unsettling experience.

Mi Aventura Ecuatoreana

One of the more bizarre statements attributed to Moe was the one in which he told Wilson in the immediate presence of Lois, Wilson's wife, that Wilson needed a more adventurous kind of woman who would share Wilson's interests. Duh? By the time that the statement was made, Moe had nearly become Wilson's shadow. I must admit, that I probably didn't make a positive contribution to our social situation by singing the words, "Me and my shadow...." whenever Wilson mentioned Moe's name in my presence, usually with an air of great frustration and concern.

You have now met our tour leader, Paul, and four members of our traveling group, Lois, Wilson, Barbara and Moe. Along with me, the group had, for the most part, enjoyed the earlier parts of our trip.

On the evening of our arrival in Quito, we were taken to La Casa del Alabado, a private museum filled with exhibits of regional Ecuadorean clothing, weapons, shaman tools, and other items of historical and cultural interest. After a brief tour of about three or four floors we were ushered into a room of the museum in which dinner was served.

Fortunately, there was no additional drama until we returned to the Hotel Reina Isabel and I was in my room changing into sleeping gear. I looked down at my right lower leg and was a bit shocked at what I saw. From my knee to the toes on my right leg, swelling had reached the point that the entire lower limb was about a third larger than the corresponding area on my left leg. In addition to the pronounced swelling, the lower right leg was unusually hot, especially when compared to my lower left leg.

At first, I thought that I would call the tour director about my newly discovered condition. Soon afterwards, counter-ideas popped into my head and I decided that I would wait until morning to see whether my condition was fleeting. If not, I had to get medical attention. I pretty much knew that I was experiencing a blood clot or thrombotic event. Wishful thinking supported my delay. After all, 2013 had already brought about a mini-disaster of a diagnosis for me, advanced prostate cancer with lymph node involvement. This diagnosis was made in March 2013. It was, therefore, probably wrong of me to even think that the universe had made a mistake and was allowing yet another mini-disaster to occur in my life before I had fully overcome the damage done to my bowels and bladder by 44 days of pelvic radiation therapy. Besides which, maybe the swelling was a consequence of sitting too long in too many airports and airplane seats during this trip to Bolivia, Colombia, and Ecuador.

After a pretty sleepless night, I waited until about 6 a.m. on Saturday to call Paul. Passing of the night did absolutely nothing to change the look of my swollen foot, ankle, and calf. About 20 minutes after my call, Paul and I were in a taxi en route to the nearest hospital. The emergency room staff put me through the usual battery of tests -chest x-ray, e.k.g., sonogram of right thigh and leg, blood tests, etc. After about 3 hours or so, the diagnosis was confirmed, DEEP VEIN THROMBOSIS! I would have to be hospitalized for a few days.

An i.v. solution was started. Added to medication given in the emergency room was my first dose of Enoxaparin (Lovenox), a blood thinner. A nurse had me cover my particulars and roll up my hospital gown. After an antiseptic swab of the area, she grabbed a handful of abdominal fat and fired away with the pre-filled syringe of the drug. At last, a useful purpose of belly fat.

In the mean time, I lost Paul's services as interpreter. He had to leave me around 7:30 a.m. in order to lead the rest of our group into the additional destinations called for in our schedule. So, for about an hour, I had to muddle through as best as I could because no one in the emergency room spoke English. I have already described my very highly limited Spanish language skills. Fatima, another rep from the travel company responsible for our travel success and well-being, did show up about an hour or so after Paul departed. Needless to say, I was more than happy to see her.

Before leaving the emergency room and prior to being admitted, I was given a choice of an ordinary patient room or a suite for an extra $248 dollars per day. I chose a suite because I thought that it would buy me an extra level of privacy and comfort. Finally, the young man who had wheeled me from the emergency room to the various specialty exams wheeled me to my waiting suite on the third floor in another section of the hospital. Naturally, I assumed that the quality of the food would match my elevated choice of accommodations. Reality would rear its slightly ugly head a bit later on.

Even though my recall of the succession of events immediately after admission has already gotten cloudy, it is clear that El Senor Doctor Miguel Gomez became the physician responsible for my care. I did get across to him during our first meeting that, "Soy farmaceutico jubilado." I am a retired pharmacist. He smiled on hearing that statement coming from me. Apparently, he passed along my status to the nursing staff.

So, it should not have been a surprise when I began to question the identity of any medication that I was about to be given. I found out that a white pill that I had been given earlier was paracetamol, or the equivalent of a Tylenol (strength unknown). Later, I advised the nurses that my 1 liter i.v. bag was empty. Close scrutiny of the label revealed that the bag had contained normal saline with the addition of 10meq. potassium chloride. On another occasion, a nurse brought another white pill for me to take. "Que es esta medicina?" Said I. "Amlodipina" said the nurse. I explained that I had already taken my increased daily dose of amlodipine from my personal supply. In addition to everything else, my blood pressure had begun to drift upwards and beyond control. Between the usual array of old people's regimens for high blood pressure, high cholesterol, etc., I now had to take additional prophylaxis medicines for prevention of night sweats caused by either chronic obstructive sleep apnea (diagnosed about 4 years earlier) or extended side effects from leuprolide, an anti-testosterone hormone therapy that was intended to get my maleness stuff down to immeasurable levels. Apparently, leuprolide was also responsible for reducing the size of my testicles, the dimensions of which were nothing to write home about even before the cancer treatment started. Now I have to conduct special search and observe missions just to prove to myself that I still got a pair. But, I digress (again).

Getting back to the exclusivity conferred by the suite, it was exclusive in one easily observed way. I never saw another patient on the third floor until I was being discharged.

So, there was certainly no mixing of Real Ecuadoreans with Gringo types such as yours truly. Okay, I did not learn whether there were special terms that were applied to Gringos who looked like me. Afro-Ecuadoreans make up a very tiny portion of the population. That phrase, looking like me, brings up another observation. All of the nurses realized finally, that I was an American because so many of them had asked me the same question, "De donde eres?" To each inquirer, I had proudly responded that I was from Los Estados Unidos, el estado de la Florida. Usually, the response was, "La Florida!"

A number of things occurred to me regarding the differences in nursing practices in the U.S. versus those that I observed at El Hospital Clinicas de Pichincha. (For your edification dear reader, Pichincha is the name of the region in which Quito is located.) Of the most glaring differences was the observation that nurses never wore latex gloves even while managing intravenous (i.v.) sites and flushing intravenous lines. At one point, a bag of i.v. pantoprazole had emptied and blood had begun to flow backwards from my arm and into the i.v. tubing. A gloveless nurse took care of the problem. This technique would not have been allowed in the U.S. because it provided an opportunity for blood-borne pathogens or germs to be transmitted from patient to nurse and probably patient to nurse to another patient. Glass oral thermometers were reused repeatedly after only a tap water rinse. It was unclear whether used oral thermometers were reused after a patient was discharged. Fortunately, no rectal temps were required.

Nurses never revealed the names of medications before attempting to administer them. Medications were prepared away from my bedside. There was no reliable way that an oral medication could be positively identified at bedside by the nurse before its administration. A white pill is a white pill is a white pill. I also got the feeling that nurses were not accustomed to being challenged by the patient whenever some new medication appeared.

Well into the second day of my hospitalization, I began to suspect that there were at least two different agendas at work insofar as the nursing staff was concerned. One was the nurses' responses in following Dr. Miguel Gomez's orders; the other had to do with the apparent curiosity that most of the nursing staff exhibited towards me. At one point, one of the nurses said something about the color of my skin and the color of my eyes. She gave this kind of smile/leer after she had said it and then exited the suite.

My immediate thought was, "Oh gosh! Here we go again.". Starting in early childhood with my older sister Margaret, then later, classmates in elementary school, I had to endure taunts like, "Here kitty kitty!" or statements like, "You have cat eyes." The ultimate taunt was "You ole cat eyes, you!" Then there was my younger sister's epiphany around age 3 or 4. She must have looked into my eyes for the first time in her life. She yelled, "Mama! Mama! Junior's got eyes like Frisco." Frisco was the dog that lived with relatives across the street. Did I mention before that I was called Junior while growing up? Junior Mills when there needed to be distinctions between other Juniors in the neighborhood. Then, there were some other people who found my eye color (hazel) attractive. Even my skin color had previously drawn favorable attention. At one hospital where I worked for several years, one nurse rather admiringly pointed out the level of "orange" pigmentation in my skin. (Okay, I know that there is no quasi-orange melanin component responsible for my skin color, but here it is a descriptor). Well, being the good guy that I am, I did not disabuse her of the notion of "orangeness" even though I would have preferred use of the word, copper. After all, I have used the word, copper, in describing my paternal great grandfather's skin color. No matter. Here was a nurse who was placing me in the category of a piece of exotica if I read the situation correctly.

Maybe, just maybe, there was a connection between being perceived as somewhat exotic and an event that occurred a bit later on. Before breakfast, a nurse came into my room and asked whether I wanted to shower before breakfast or afterwards. I expressed my preference for afterwards. She did indeed come back after I had disposed of the semi-cold hard-boiled egg and had polished off the semi-warm soup (always a variant of potato soup, for reasons that were never clear.) and the lukewarm coffee. At no point during my hospital stay was I served a hot meal nor had a hot cup of coffee. It became clear that one of the anticipated advantages of being in a suite in El Hospital Clinicas de Pichincha was certainly neither food quality nor variety.

Well, the nurse who followed up on my showering preferences left after turning on the shower and adjusting the water temperature. She had unhooked me from the i.v. pole and bag and I was free to go. I decided that I wanted/needed a bit of skin left over so I did not stay under the shower too long. Seconds after stepping out from the shower and I was drying off, there was a rap on the door. Next (only a second or two later), the bathroom door flew open and there were three nurses standing in the bathroom doorway smiling and greeting me with various "Holas", "Como esta usted?", etc. Fortunately, at the moment in which the door burst open, my towel was covering my nether regions. Accordingly, if there were indeed conspiratorial efforts to observe all of me, this occasion was not going to be one of them. My hand continued to hold steady until they exited. I would continue to hold on to my secret as to how unkind nature had been to me. After all, why should I single handedly destroy a stereotype that was, in some ways, based upon overblown assumptions?

Surprisingly, I was not at all rattled by this significant invasion of my privacy. Having been admitted with no spare clothes of my own, I resigned myself to endure the typical "camisa" with the opening down the back that remained open no matter how many times that I grabbed a hand full of the gown so as not to reveal my rear end to any and all intentional or accidental observers. Trying to effect this "face-saving" measure while waltzing around guiding a reluctantly mobile i.v. pole was quite a challenge. Another breach in privacy occurred when I was in the bathroom with the door closed, posing on the throne as did Rodin's "The Thinker". There was a rap on the door, the door immediately flew open and the maid, less than 3 feet away, looked up at me and said, "Disculpe". (Excuse me.) She quickly removed the waste basket and shut the door. HEY, I'M AN AMERICAN! SOME THINGS LIKE PERSONAL SPACE ARE SACRED! It became apparent that Ecuadoreans and Americans have very distinct differences in what is considered good manners, personal space and privacy.

My experiences in trying to communicate with the nursing staff and Dr. Gomez, despite our respective language barriers and limitations were a lot of fun. I got so involved trying to conjure up simple but applicable Spanish words and phrases in order to crack a joke or respond appropriately that it chewed up a lot of my time. Also, I had no reading material for the first time on this trip. My books were packed in my luggage under temporary storage in the Hotel Isabel La Reina.

It was really comical when one of the nurses decided that I would understand Spanish much more clearly if she spoke louder and much more slowly. Now, where had I heard of that technique before? Every now and then, my ego became swollen when I tried to crack a joke in Spanish and was rewarded with a laugh or a grin on the face of my intended audience member(s). Of course, they

127

also could have been smiling or laughing because the joke was so bad.

Despite the suddenness of the hospitalization, I did have my camera with me after I was admitted. So, on the morning of day number four, discharge day, I took a picture of both shifts of nurses, nurses coming on duty and those going off duty. One of the young physicians who wandered into the room while all of the noise of directions, and orders, and instructions were going on offered to shoot a picture of me standing with all of the nurses, including the nursing supervisor (La Jefa). Although I had no direct evidence, I suspected that few other patients brought along a camera and used it to photograph members of the nursing staff as if we were having some type of celebratory event. I had also told a couple of the nurses that I was going to write a short story (una historia corta) about my experiences in Quito when I returned home and I would title the story, Mi Aventura Ecuatoreana.

For certain, one sure reason for celebrating on day four was that the swelling in my leg had all but disappeared. Indeed, a measurement of both calves showed only a one centimeter difference in right and left legs. All of my other signs were normal. I was so appreciative of this reality it made me more determined to "get out of Dodge" and get to my family physician back in Gainesville, Florida, my hometown. I wanted to be declared totally recovered by someone in whom I had a lot of faith over at least a couple of decades. Besides which, in addition to being a highly competent physician, Dr. Black always wanted to know about my latest travels. This type of interest will get and/or seal my loyalty every time.

Between Grand Circle Travel's Quito office personnel and the travel insurance company's cooperation, I arrived back in Gainesville a day early on Thursday morning after having been discharged from El Hospital Clinicas de Pichincha on Tuesday afternoon. I was given a bulkhead seat in business class on Delta's non-stop flight from Quito to Atlanta. The same was true of my short hop from Atlanta to Gainesville. No medical issues occurred while en route.

It has occurred to me that during my hospital stay, I spent practically no time at all agonizing about my medical condition or the double whammy of two very serious ailments happening within such a short span of time - advanced prostate cancer and deep vein thrombosis both within a six month period. It is possible that the gratitude thing had finally begun to kick in. For so many years, I focused on those things and conditions which I felt that I did not have but wanted. I spent a lot of time wallowing in self-pity and being angry because I saw myself as having been short-changed in life. Often, I felt that my emotional state was not only poverty stricken but the levels of poverty in my heart and mind were also pretty high.

Now, my daily prayer involves giving thanks to The Creator for each gift that I receive or have received during the course of my life, petitioning for the wisdom and discipline to hone those gifts which will help me to improve the quality of my own life and to positively impact the lives of others. By George, I think it's working!

I owe a huge chunk of thanks to Paul, Veronica, Fatima, and Victoria (program services manager) all from the Grand Circle office in Quito - for all of their help in periodically bridging the language gap for me, especially at certain moments of the process. Things went a lot more smoothly for me when one of these folks was around. Also, I would be totally remiss if I didn't say, "THANK YOU." to my fellow travelers during all three phases of the trip, Bolivia, Colombia, and Ecuador. It is hard to imagine that a better and more enjoyable group could be found anywhere else on the planet. I have coined a name for this small group of well-traveled folks, The BCE Travelers. You know, Bolivia, Columbia, and Ecuador. Members of this group have traveled to so many parts of the globe that they can no longer be classified as tourists. Instead, they should rightfully be called travelers. Much to my surprise (being the introvert that I claim to be), I invited Barbara G., Lois, and Wilson to visit me in Gainesville for six days at the end of February 2014. In my many years of group travel, I have never felt such genuine connectedness towards any fellow-travelers before. It is very clear that Wilson collects people as a magnet collects iron particles. Lois, his wife, is the quieter force that, among many other family duties, keeps Wilson grounded, in my opinion. Barbara G. appears to be the epitome of Southern womanhood without the prejudices and biases. Oh! Did I mention that I am a native Southern black and that Lois, Wilson, and Barbara are Caucasian? No matter. More power to all of the BCE Travelers. Keep on truckin' guys!